INNOVATIVE
TECHNOLOGIES

HYBRID AND ELECTRIC VEHICLES

ABDO
Publishing Company

INNOVATIVE TECHNOLOGIES

HYBRID AND ELECTRIC VEHICLES

BY L. E. CARMICHAEL

CONTENT CONSULTANT

Andrew Frank

Professor Emeritus, Mechanical and Aeronautical Engineering

University of California-Davis and CTO of Efficient Drivetrains Inc.

CREDITS

Published by ABDO Publishing Company, PO Box 398166, Minneapolis, MN 55439. Copyright © 2013 by Abdo Consulting Group, Inc. International copyrights reserved in all countries. No part of this book may be reproduced in any form without written permission from the publisher. The Essential Library™ is a trademark and logo of ABDO Publishing Company.

Printed in the United States of America,
North Mankato, Minnesota

102012
012013

 THIS BOOK CONTAINS AT LEAST 10% RECYCLED MATERIALS.

Editor: Rebecca Felix
Series Designer: Craig Hinton

Photo Credits: Fedor Selivanov/Shutterstock Images, cover; Shutterstock Images, 6, 30, 34, 42, 61, 64, 84; Con Tanasuik/Design Pics/Thinkstock, 9; Thinkstock, 11, 97; Sjoerd van der Wal/iStockphoto, 14; Hulton Archive/Getty Images, 16; AP Images, 19; James H. Hare/Library of Congress, 23; Henry Burroughs/AP Images, 27; Encyclopedia Britannica/UIG/Getty Images, 33; Douglas Healey/AP Images, 39; Dorling Kindersley/DK Images, 45; Red Line Editorial, 46, 58–59, 86 ; Stan Honda/AFP/Getty Images, 51; Darren Brode/Shutterstock Images, 54; Jeffrey MacMillan/The Washington Post/Getty Images, 69; Daniel Acker/Bloomberg/Getty Images, 74; Bill Pugliano/Getty Images, 79; Jacquelyn Martin/AP Images, 82; Darryl Dyck/The Canadian Press/AP Images, 91; Anthony Baggett/iStockphoto, 94; Shizuo Kambayashi/AP Images, 100

Library of Congress Cataloging-in-Publication Data
Carmichael, L. E. (Lindsey E.)
  Hybrid and electric vehicles / L.E. Carmichael.
    pages cm. -- (Innovative technologies)
  Includes bibliographical references.
  ISBN 978-1-61783-463-9
1. Hybrid electric cars--Juvenile literature. I. Title.
  TL221.15.C37 2013
  629.22'93--dc23
                        2012023991

>> TABLE OF CONTENTS

CHAPTER 1

RUNNING ON FUMES

Global warming. The greenhouse effect. No matter what you call it, most scientists agree the earth's climate is changing. This is mostly due to the concentration of carbon dioxide in the atmosphere, which traps heat. That concentration started increasing during the Industrial Revolution of the nineteenth century, when people began burning fossil fuels such as coal, oil, and natural gas. The concentration has been rising since then. According to measurements made by the Earth System Research Laboratory in Hawaii, atmospheric carbon dioxide rose by approximately 24 percent from 1959 to 2010.[1]

One major source of carbon dioxide is exhaust from gasoline and diesel fuel–powered vehicles. When gasoline burns, carbon within combines with oxygen in the air to form carbon dioxide, which is emitted through the vehicle's tailpipe. Carbon

« **Car exhaust from gasoline and diesel contributes to global warming by increasing carbon dioxide emissions.**

POLLUTANTS IN PETROL

Internal combustion engine (ICE) emissions include:

- Carbon dioxide (CO_2), a greenhouse gas
- Carbon monoxide (CO), a poisonous gas
- Ozone (O_3) and nitrogen oxide (NOx), which cause breathing problems
- Sulfur oxide (SOx), a mixture of several compounds that contribute to acid rain
- Nitrous oxides (NOx), a major contributor to acid rain
- Volatile organic compounds (VOCs), which contribute to smog

dioxide emissions contribute to global warming, including the heating of the atmosphere and the melting of global ice. Worldwide, approximately 83 million short tons (75 million metric tons) of carbon are released into the atmosphere every day.[2] And 5 percent of that—4.13 million short tons (3.75 million metric tons)—comes from vehicles driven in the United States.[3]

Carbon dioxide can damage lung health and affect breathing. In addition to carbon dioxide, vehicle exhaust contains carbon monoxide and volatile organic compounds (VOCs). Carbon monoxide and VOCs react with sunlight and create ozone, which in part makes up smog. High concentrations of carbon monoxide can be toxic to humans. Smog is a visual haze of pollution present in the air of many large cities. Ozone naturally belongs high up in the atmosphere, where it benefits humans by filtering out the ultraviolet radiation responsible for sunburns and other skin damage. However, when emitted as a part of car exhaust at ground level, ozone

In addition to being unsightly, smog can be dangerous to human health.

irritates the lungs, making it difficult for people to breathe—especially for those with health problems such as asthma.

Exhaust emissions are not the only downside of driving traditional gas and diesel vehicles, which are also known as internal combustion engine (ICE) vehicles. The gasoline and diesel that fuels these vehicles comes from oil, which is a fossil fuel. Fossil fuels develop from the decomposition of organic materials such as plants and animals that were buried beneath layers of earth and rock. It takes millions of years for these organic materials to develop into fossil fuels such as coal, natural gas, and oil, from which gasoline and diesel are derived. Finding and mining new deposits of these resources is expensive and often damaging to the environment.

In 1956 M. King Hubbert, a geologist for the global fossil fuels company Shell, argued that the rate of oil production would change over time. As people discovered new deposits, the rate of production would increase until it reached a maximum, or peak. Then, once less oil remained to be discovered, production would slow until it hit zero when the oil was completely used up. This idea is now known as Hubbert's Peak, or peak oil. Estimates of the total amount of oil in the world have increased, and we've developed new ways to extract it. But despite this, many people believe that Hubbert's Peak has already been reached, and that oil production will now start to slow down, which will cause oil to become more and more expensive.

Refining oil to create fuels produces harmful carbon emissions. As demand for fuel increases, more oil is refined and more pollution created.

Yet even as we may be running out of oil, our demand for it is increasing. A 2008 study at the University of California, Davis, estimated that oil consumption rises by approximately 1.3 percent every year, and that oil would therefore be used up by the year 2041.[4] These numbers cause concern for many who feel oil is not a dependable energy source for the future.

Of the 1.3 trillion gallons (4.9 trillion liters) of oil the United States uses every year, two-thirds, or roughly 871 billion gallons (3.3 trillion liters), is converted to fuel for vehicles.[5] The rest is used to create energy for heating and electricity. Between 1950 and 2000, the earth's population doubled; during this same time period, the number of cars increased tenfold.[6]

Many countries, including the United States, do not have enough oil to support their energy needs, and so their oil must largely be sourced from foreign countries. But even foreign oil amounts are limited. As more countries need more oil, the amount available to any one nation decreases. That's one reason why gasoline prices are increasing. The rising expense of foreign oil often hinges on dependency. Being dependent on foreign countries for oil creates instability and an increase in price if the supply is threatened. That's exactly what happened in 1973 and 1974, when the Organization of Petroleum Exporting Countries (OPEC) decided not to sell oil to the United States for political reasons. This created an energy crisis: the price of gas rose and the US economy took a nosedive. In the years since, it's estimated that price hikes and interruptions in foreign oil supplies have cost the United States $7 trillion.[7]

One way to break dependency on foreign oil and diminish air pollution is using alternative vehicles that greatly decrease or completely eliminate the need for gasoline. These alternatives include innovative ICE vehicles that run on fuel other than fossil fuels, electric vehicles (EVs) that run solely on electricity, and hybrid vehicles, which are powered by two distinct power sources, often electric power combined with another source, such as gasoline. Plug-in hybrid electric vehicles (PHEVs), which are essentially hybrid electric vehicles (HEVs) that have larger batteries charged with electricity independent from the vehicle, are another option.

In addition to being a cleaner option, hybrid and electric vehicles are often more efficient than traditional ICE vehicles, using less approximate measures of energy per mile. As the sole power source for a vehicle, however, electricity has some drawbacks, including expense, convenience, and range. Many hybrid vehicles share these drawbacks, in addition to having others, such as still needing a second power source, which is often gasoline or other liquid fuels.

The concepts of hybrid and electric vehicles are not new. Alternative vehicles have been on the road as long as their gasoline-dependent counterparts. But today's researchers are working not only to level any shortcomings that hybrids and electrics have in comparison to

A BIG GOAL

The Intergovernmental Panel on Climate Change is calling for an 80 percent global reduction in greenhouse gas emissions by 2050. Since new innovations take time to replace existing technology, this goal can be met only if alternative vehicles can be mass-produced at reasonable prices by the year 2030. But Sweden doesn't even want to wait that long: its goal is to free its economy of oil by 2020. China has also become increasingly more aggressive in switching to alternative fuels and vehicles since they now import more oil than the United States.

traditional vehicles, but to also surpass them by miles. Innovative models are being created that are not only cleaner, more powerful, and more efficient than their predecessors, but that are also likely to capture drivers' imaginations in ways vehicles have never done before.

These vehicles might even save the world. Engineer student Andrew Shabashevich certainly thinks so. "This is why we work so many hours on [these projects]," he says. "We think this is the right path for the future of the world—one where we actually have a future."[8]

≪ Exciting innovations to alternative vehicles, such as plug-in hybrid electric vehicles, focus on improving efficiency and reducing pollution.

THE HORSELESS CARRIAGE

During the nineteenth century, most vehicles were pulled by horses. Horse-drawn buggies, trucks, and carts were used to transport everything from people to milk to garbage. Horse power was effective, but hardly ideal. Horses were noisy, hungry, easily startled, and vulnerable to weather and disease. They were also dirty. An 1899 article in *Scientific American* magazine estimated that in New York City alone, 1,600 men were employed full-time removing horse manure from the streets.[1]

Fortunately, scientists at the turn of the century in Europe and North America were experimenting with a new form of transportation: the horseless carriage. These revolutionary vehicles were considered "environmental godsends" that would solve all of the problems of horse power.[2] Three main types of propulsion were used in these new vehicles: steam, gasoline, and electricity.

 Nicolas-Joseph Cugnot's steam powered vehicle, 1771

STEAM

The first self-propelled vehicle, built for use by the French army by Nicolas-Joseph Cugnot in 1769, was powered by steam. Soon inventors in both Europe and North America were experimenting with steam engines for general transportation. These early cars burned wood or coal to produce steam until liquid fuel was invented in 1859. By 1903, more than 2,100 of the 4,000 vehicles registered in New York State were steam powered.[3]

Steamers, as these vehicles were known, were cheap to fuel and could reach speeds of up to 127 miles per hour (204 km/h).[4] Unfortunately, they also had some drawbacks. High temperatures were required to produce the steam that powered them, and their kerosene or gasoline burners took a long time to warm up. In addition, their boilers ran dry after an approximate 150 miles (240 km). Drivers refilled them using existing public horse-watering troughs, but these were removed in 1914 when foot-and-mouth disease broke out among American livestock. The removal of the public troughs during this outbreak made it difficult for drivers to refill their boilers while traveling. Due to these limitations, steam-powered vehicles had all but disappeared by 1930.

GASOLINE

During the mid-nineteenth century, oil was used in the United States primarily for making kerosene, which was burned in lamps. Gasoline was a byproduct of the kerosene production process and was believed to have little value. Then, during the late 1870s, German inventor Nikolas Otto developed a four-stroke ICE powered by burning this inexpensive and portable fuel. His ICE used the pressure of exploding gases to drive pistons, thus creating motion. Rudolf Diesel quickly followed on Otto's heels, developing an advanced engine that ignited the fuel automatically and burned less refined fuels. Otto's engine quickly became the standard design, however, and is the ICE still in use today. When massive oil deposits were found in Texas in 1901, gasoline became even cheaper and easier to purchase, making ICE vehicles a popular choice for drivers.

By the 1920s, road surfaces on rural highways had improved dramatically, launching a new craze known as touring. Suddenly it was not only possible, but also fashionable, for Americans to travel from city to city. Drivers of ICE cars could fill up with gas almost anywhere—in towns without filling stations, stores even sold it in jars and jugs. There were few limits on how far a gasoline-powered vehicle could take its drivers.

Not everything about these cars was favorable, however. For instance, to start the vehicle, the driver had to rotate a lever, or crank, in order to create combustion in the engine. It was difficult and dangerous work: if the engine backfired or the driver lost his grip, the crank could spin, breaking his arm. Another disadvantage of internal combustion vehicles was that they created pollution—both exhaust that was harmful to people and the environment and noise caused by their clattering, rattling moving parts. When ICEs were introduced, many people felt the air and noise pollution they created would eventually become as offensive as the piles of horse manure they replaced.

ELECTRICITY

Vehicles powered by batteries were another option for early motorists. The first such vehicle powered by electricity was a tricycle invented by Frenchman Gustave Trouvé in 1881. Nine years later, Andrew L. Riker built the first electric tricycle in the United States. He soon switched to making four-wheel vehicles.

EVs ran quietly and without vibrations or exhaust. Perhaps most important, they could be turned on by flicking a switch. Because of these advantages, EVs quickly became the most popular type of horseless carriage. Between 1899 and 1900, which was the height of early competition between these vehicles, 38 percent of new cars sold were electric—more than any other type.[4] Several major cities, including New York City, began using fleets of electric taxicabs. Even Clara Ford, the wife of Ford Motor Company founder Henry Ford, drove an electric car in 1914, saying she found her husband's gas cars made too much noise.

ELECTRICS AIM AT WOMEN

An article in a 1904 edition of *Outing* magazine claimed that motoring came naturally to a man, whereas, "The only thing about a car which a woman does not have to teach herself . . . is how to dress for it."[5] The makers of EVs took a different view. At the peak of the electric's popularity, which was between about 1895 and 1915, car advertisements pictured women three times more often than men.[6] For their part, women loved EVs, which gave them the freedom to travel on their own.

O nly 10,000 people fit in the grandstands, but that hasn't stopped another 40,000 from crowding around the oval track. It's 5:30 p.m. on September 7 in Narragansett Park, and the most anticipated event of the Rhode Island State Fair is about to begin.

Seven cars are pulled up at the starting line. Each bears a driver and a passenger, who is acting as the required cargo weight. The race also has a minimum speed limit, and vehicles that can't maintain it will be disqualified.

At the pole position on the inside edge, Andrew Riker sits in the car he invented, gazing at the course. It is a mile's (1.6 km) worth of rough and lumpy dirt, and there's a strong wind blowing. The point of the race is to show what these vehicles can do, but will Riker be able to reach top speed under such unfavorable conditions?

There's no more time to wonder. The starter cries out for the drivers to go, and the race is on. Riker's car immediately pulls into the lead. Only one other vehicle is even close to him. He speeds around the track and comes "dashing over the finish line, his body bent forward as though holding the reigns over some spirited steed."[7] The crowd shouts and cheers, and as his winning car rolls to a stop, people rush forward for a closer look.

Andrew Riker in an early automobile race

It's a beautifully designed vehicle with leather seats and wheels like a bicycle's. Without passengers, it weighs 1,500 pounds (680 kg). Eight hundred of those pounds (363 kg) come from batteries, because Riker's car doesn't run on gasoline. It runs on electricity, and with an average speed of 24 miles per hour (39 km/h), it's just defeated five gas-powered vehicles in the first track-run automobile race in the United States.[8]

The year is 1896. Riker has no idea that, a century from now, electric cars will still be the vehicles of the future. But he'd probably be thrilled to know that scientists, engineers, and researchers are doing everything they can to make that future happen.

Another benefit of electric motors was that they had very few moving parts. Unlike ICE engines, they seldom broke down or needed maintenance. However, electric motors relied on batteries, which produce electricity via chemical reactions. Because those reactions took place in a liquid, the batteries sometimes froze during winter. Even if the battery did not freeze, the chemical reaction became less efficient when the temperature dropped, meaning the car could not be driven as far or as fast.

And winter or summer, batteries ran out of electric charge, just as ICE vehicles ran out of gas. To recharge a battery, the vehicle had to be plugged in. But few private homes had electricity before World War I, so automakers, battery manufacturers, and utility companies offered alternatives. In 1900 in New York City, for instance, General Electric installed parking-meter-style hydrants known as electrants. Customers could insert coins into these electrants to buy a certain amount of charging time. But since regaining full charge took several hours, some businesses offered rental programs. Customers leased the battery at a fixed rate and mileage and could swap their dead batteries for fresh ones and be driving again in minutes.

Despite these innovations, charging stations and battery exchange stations were expensive to build and difficult to find outside of larger cities. Since most electric vehicles could go less than 100 miles (161 km) before their batteries required charging, their popularity faded when the touring craze began to catch on.

EARLY HYBRIDS

Early inventors tackled electric vehicles' range problem by building hybrids. The idea was that, with a gasoline engine to help, an electric vehicle could keep going even after its battery ran low. The first hybrid is thought to have been created by an Italian named Count Felix Carli in 1894. Belgian engineer and race car driver Camille Jenatzy took the hybrid concept one step further in 1903. He connected the gas engine of his hybrid to a generator that charged the car's battery while the car was driven.

American inventors designed hybrids too, but none of these cars sold very well. Because they were heavier than gasoline cars, hybrids were also slower, maxing out around 30 miles per hour (48 km/h).[9] In comparison, the gasoline-run 1908 Ford Model T Tourer had a top speed of 42 miles per hour (68 km/h).[10]

The price tag was the biggest drawback for both hybrids and electrics. It cost between $1,750 and $3,000 (approximately $40,000 and $67,000 in 2010) to buy a new EV in 1912. A hybrid vehicle might cost as much as $6,500. That price was ten times the price of a gas-powered Model T Ford. Because the electricity to recharge cost more than gasoline, EVs were also more expensive to run at the time.

In 1912, the first automatic starter was installed on a gas-powered Cadillac, eliminating the need for crank starts. With this innovation, the ICE vehicle became as easy to start as an electric, in addition to being cheaper, easier to refuel, and free of range restrictions. With so many advantages over electrics and hybrids, ICE-powered cars rapidly became the standard in vehicle technology.

MOVING TOWARD TODAY'S VEHICLES

By 1930, alternative vehicles had nearly disappeared, but they would soon make a comeback. During World War II (1939 to 1945), England used electrics for garbage collection and milk delivery, saving gas for military efforts. But when the war ended and oil became widely available again, people returned to gasoline-powered engines. This pattern continued during the second half of the twentieth century. Interest in alternative vehicles increased whenever concerns about oil prices and pollution peaked, and decreased when those concerns faded.

President Lyndon Johnson signs the Clean Air Act in 1963, which set a precedent for mandated pollution control and became more aggressive through future amendments.

Over the last few decades, such concerns have been on the rise once again. As interest in hybrids and electrics increases, improvements to gas-powered vehicles have been made as well. For example, in 1970, the US Congress passed amendments to the Clean Air Act of 1963, demanding new automobiles produce 90 percent fewer emissions by 1975.

The Corporate Average Fuel Economy (CAFE) standards for vehicle gas mileage were also established in 1975, after the OPEC energy crisis. The fuel economy for ICE vehicles doubled as a result.[11] This was a good start, but it was not nearly enough. The United States has one of the lowest standards for fuel economy in the world. The projected US goal set by President Barack Obama was for every car sold in the United States to get 35.5 miles per gallon (mpg) (13 km/L) by 2016, which would be a 40 percent improvement over standards in 2012.[12] The new standard is 54.5 mpg (19 km/L) by 2030.

Important efforts are being made to improve conventional gas-powered vehicles, and major breakthroughs in vehicle technology have also introduced new concepts and innovations in electrics and hybrids. With innovations like PHEVs and fuel cell vehicles under development since the late 1960s, the future of the transportation world may face sweeping changes. In order

CLEAN AIR ACT AND CATALYTIC CONVERTERS

The Clean Air Act of 1970 resulted in an invention called a catalytic converter by John Mooney and Carl Keith in 1975. Catalytic converters are located on the exhaust line between the engine and the tailpipe. Their purpose is to prevent dangerous emissions from leaving the vehicle by first converting them to less-harmful chemicals. For instance, emissions of nitrogen oxides, which are harmful pollutants, are converted to nitrogen, a natural component of air. Carbon monoxide and VOCs react with additional oxygen, forming carbon dioxide.

Carbon dioxide emissions are still problematic, but some consider carbon dioxide less harmful to health than VOCs and carbon monoxide. Carbon dioxide reductions are usually achieved by increasing fuel economy, or the number of miles a vehicle can travel on a single gallon of gasoline, by decreasing the amount of gasoline a vehicle uses. Since its invention in 1975, all new ICE cars use a catalytic converter.

for alternative vehicles to address the downfalls of earlier vehicle models, researchers must first understand how traditional vehicles fit into the technological world and transition seamlessly to a future alternative starting from the current energy supply distribution system.

INTERNAL COMBUSTION ENGINE VEHICLES

With remarkable innovations being made in the world of hybrid and electric vehicles, fresh ideas for ICE vehicles will be important if they are to remain a relevant form of transportation in the future. To develop innovations in efficiency and test new fuels, researchers must first have a complete understanding of how these engines work.

HOW AN ICE WORKS

An ICE is a device for turning the chemical energy stored in gasoline into mechanical energy—the motion of the wheels that propels the vehicle. Making this happen requires a specific sequence of events.

When you turn the key of a gasoline-powered car, an electric switch is activated. The switch sends electricity from the small starting battery to a small electric motor.

 Internal combustion engine inside a gasoline-powered vehicle

FOUR-STROKE INTERNAL COMBUSTION ENGINE

Most gasoline vehicles use Otto's four-stroke engine, named for the number of times metal rods called pistons move through an engine's cylinders, or hollow tubes, to complete one cycle:

1. **INTAKE STROKE**

   The cycle starts with the intake stroke, in which the piston moves to the bottom of the cylinder. The intake valve opens, letting a mixture of air and gasoline into the empty space.

2. **COMPRESSION STROKE**

   On the compression stroke, the piston shoots up into the cylinder, compressing the fuel mixture. This compression lends the combustion more power.

3. **POWER STROKE**

   As the piston reaches the top, the spark plug sends electricity from the battery into the cylinder, igniting the fuel. The fuel explodes, producing gas and heat. The gas expands, forcing the piston down.

4. **EXHAUST STROKE**

   As the piston moves back up again, it pushes the gases out through the exhaust valve. They then exit the car through the tailpipe.

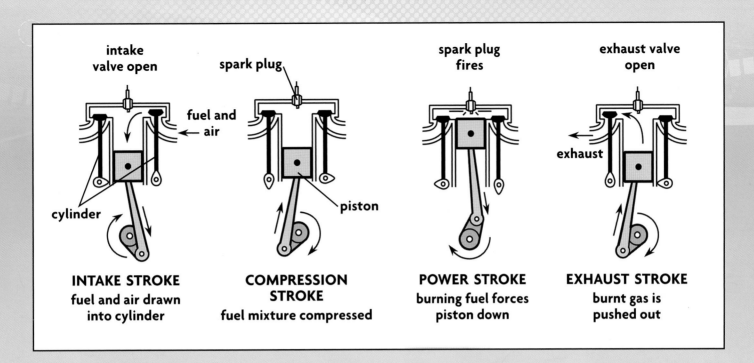

intake valve open

spark plug

fuel and air ←

cylinder

piston

INTAKE STROKE
fuel and air drawn
into cylinder

**COMPRESSION
STROKE**
fuel mixture compressed

spark plug fires

POWER STROKE
burning fuel forces
piston down

exhaust valve open

exhaust

EXHAUST STROKE
burnt gas is
pushed out

Current vehicle engines usually have at least four pistons, each at a different stage of the cycle when the engine is running. Each piston attaches to a crankshaft, which converts the pistons' up-and-down motion into circular rotational motion. As the crankshaft turns, it moves the gears of the transmission. The transmission connects to the driveshaft that powers the wheels.

Diesel engines also use internal combustion, but function slightly different than gasoline ICEs. In a gasoline ICE, fuel and air are mixed before they are compressed to create combustion. In a diesel ICE, the air is compressed *before* the fuel is added. Diesel is also made from oil and produces carbon emissions from being burned just as gasoline does.

This motor doesn't move the car. It is the mechanism that replaced the hand cranks of early vehicles. It turns over the engine and begins the firing that burns the gasoline, which then creates motion via combustion.

FUEL ISSUES

The gasoline ICE is the type most commonly used in vehicles. Gasoline and oil have a high energy density, meaning small amounts pack a lot of power. Despite a high energy density, the pollution, political issues, and price tag associated with oil use are growing concerns for many people throughout the world. Scientists at the Massachusetts Institute of Technology believe that one of the most practical ways to reduce the fuel consumption—and carbon dioxide emissions—of gasoline- and diesel-fueled cars is to reduce their size and weight and improve their performance.[1] But these changes alone will not be enough to meet global goals for carbon dioxide emission reductions.

Many people believe that we should instead either lessen or eliminate our dependence on fossil fuels by finding alternative fuels. By 1998, the automakers known as the Big Three — General Motors (GM), Ford, and DaimlerChrysler—were spending 10 percent of their budgets to research and develop vehicles powered by alternatives to gasoline.[2] And the Environmental

Among the most common ICE fuels are gasoline and diesel, which are both derived from oil and emit carbon when burned.

Protection Agency (EPA), along with the US Department of Energy, sponsors competitions for alternatively fueled vehicles with the hope of involving university research groups.

Over the last few decades, scientists around the world have been working to develop renewable fuels that can be produced locally, burn more cleanly than gasoline, and cost less than oil.

ETHANOL

The most popular alternative to gasoline worldwide is ethanol, which is produced when yeast cells are added to sugar. Ethanol is produced in the midwestern United States using corn as a source of glucose, or crystalline sugar. Brazil, which makes enough ethanol to be energy independent, sources its glucose from sugar cane.

Ethanol is often used as E85, a blend of 85 percent ethanol and 15 percent gasoline, or E10, which is 10 percent ethanol and 90 percent gasoline. When it is burned in a flex-fuel engine, water and carbon dioxide are produced, just as with gasoline. However, plants grown for ethanol production absorb and then store carbon that already exists in the atmosphere. This means the carbon dioxide that is released when the plants are burned is actually rereleased carbon dioxide that was already in the air. Also, the carbon cycle time of ethanol—or the time it takes for the carbon dioxide to be emitted and then absorbed by plants—is thought to be only a few years. In contrast, burning fossil fuels releases carbon that has been locked away for millions of years, and which therefore would not be part of the earth's carbon cycle at all without the intervention of human technology. These points of reason are controversial, however, and are not accepted by all scientists.

FINDING FLEX FUEL

The first ethanol factory in the United States opened on October 5, 2007, in Port of Morrow in northern Oregon. Portland, also in northern Oregon, was the first major city in the US to require ethanol and biodiesel to be publicly sold.

In 2008, there were more than 7 million flex fuel vehicles driving on US roads.[5] Most run on gasoline, however, because alternative fueling stations are not yet widely available.

Another reason using ethanol as a vehicle fuel is controversial is that many people object to using plants to fuel cars when they could be used for food. Others argue that using ethanol is not a very green practice because producing the crops to manufacture it requires a huge amount of land, sometimes causing deforestation, and the use of both fertilizer and chemical pesticides, which are often applied using machines run by fossil fuels. A bigger problem is that ethanol is estimated to reduce vehicle emissions by only 15 percent, but only decreases a vehicle's mileage by 2 to 3 percent.[6]

A component of natural gas, methane is a hydrocarbon, similar to gasoline. As with the oil used to produce gasoline, our current main source of methane is fossil fuel deposits in the earth's crust. However, unlike oil, methane does not take millions of years to form from composting organic matter such as dead plants or animals. Methane forms within weeks, and is therefore considered a renewable fuel. This form of methane is called biomethane, and it can also be produced from mammal digestion and waste—in one day, one human produces the equivalent of 1/200th of a gallon of gasoline in biogas through flatulence and waste![7]

However, methane is a greenhouse gas, and, as with other hydrocarbons, burning it to power vehicles produces carbon dioxide. However, carbon dioxide is a less powerful greenhouse gas than the methane it comes from, which could be seen as an advantage. On the other hand, methane in gaseous form requires special high-pressure storage tanks and pressure regulators. And there are currently few places in North America to fill up a natural-gas tank.

VEGETABLE OIL AND BIODIESEL

Unlike gasoline engines, diesel engines can be converted to run on vegetable oil—the same stuff you use in your kitchen! Vegetable oil contains more energy per gallon than any

»

Though its use is illegal, some US drivers use vegetable oil as fuel in diesel-engine vehicles.

conventional fuel, and because it's a plant product like ethanol, it has a carbon cycle time of just a few years. However, it's currently illegal to sell or use vegetable oil for fuel in the United States. Vehicles using vegetable oil must meet the emissions standards of the Clean Air Act prior to switching to vegetable oil as fuel, and the fuel must be registered with the EPA. Vegetable oil

AIR AS FUEL?

In 2007, India's largest car manufacturer, Tata, announced a compressed-air powered vehicle known as the MiniCAT. These vehicles store air in high-pressure tanks. When released into an engine, the air expands, moving the pistons. It's the same principle that gasoline engines use, but is much greener. Under test conditions, the MiniCAT has a 185-mile (298 km) range and can reach speeds of 68 miles per hour (109 km/h).[8] As an added bonus, the exhaust air is very cold, and can actually be used to run the car's air conditioner!

There are downsides to this technology, however. Existing compressed-air cars are less efficient than battery-powered electric vehicles and—if the energy required to fill the air tanks is considered—can produce more greenhouse gas emissions than ICEs.

is not registered by the EPA, however, as the organization finds the fuel produces many of the same environmental toxins and dangers as other fuels, including odors and the risk posed to wildlife in the event of a leak.

Biodiesel—which is made by isolating fatty acids from peanut, castor, and sunflower oils or other oily plants—is a legal alternative to vegetable oil. Biodiesel is renewable and has a short carbon cycle time, and it produces almost no emissions of carbon dioxide or sulfur oxide, which is a compound that is harmful when it interacts with gases and particles in the air.

However, producing biodiesel is expensive and also requires the use of toxic chemicals. Researchers are working to change this, but it will be some time before the technology is ready.

No matter what kind of fuel they burn, however, ICEs are somewhat inefficient. On average, only approximately 15 percent of the energy stored in the fuel is actually converted into the vehicle's motion.[9] Many think a better option is to move away from the use of ICE vehicles altogether in favor of electric power.

CHAPTER 4

ELECTRIC VEHICLES

T here are two reasons many believe electric motors are a cleaner and more effective means of transportation than ICEs. First, they have 70 percent fewer moving parts.[1] As a result, EVs are more efficient: up to 90 percent of the energy they carry is converted to motion.[2] Second, electric motors don't burn fossil fuels, and therefore have no tailpipes releasing emissions. This means that as long as the energy source powering their batteries creates no emissions, they are zero-emissions vehicles.

ELECTRICITY, MAGNETS, AND MOTORS

To understand how EVs work, it is important to first understand magnets. There are two types of magnets: permanent magnets, which are the type that hold your photos to your fridge, and electromagnets. In both types, the ends of magnets are called poles.

« **Streamlined motors and zero tailpipe emissions while driving are two advantages that lead many to consider EVs green transportation.**

The north poles of two magnets will repel each other. In contrast, the north pole of one magnet will be attracted to the south pole of another.

An electromagnet is created by wrapping a wire around a piece of metal containing iron, then connecting that wire to a source of electricity. The movement of electricity through the wire creates a magnetic field with north and south poles. The only difference between an electromagnet and a permanent magnet is that electromagnets can be turned off by disconnecting the electricity.

It is also possible to change the north and south orientation of an electromagnet by changing the direction of the flow of electricity. It is this capacity that makes electric motors work. An electromagnet called an armature is mounted on an axle—a rod around which the armature can spin. A commutator, or electric switch, attached to the armature forms a connection between it and the source of electric power.

This mechanism is placed in a large permanent magnet. Because north repels north, the armature will rotate until its north end is near the south pole of the permanent magnet. Another electro magnet can be used as well, but permanent magnets are more common.

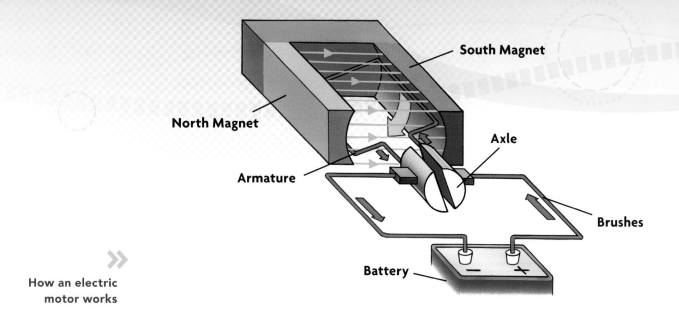

South Magnet

North Magnet

Armature

Axle

Brushes

Battery

>>
**How an electric
motor works**

At this moment, springy brushes touch the commutator, reversing the electric flow to the armature, which causes the poles of the electromagnet to reverse. Because south is now near south, the armature will rotate half a turn. This cycle is repeated until the armature begins to spin freely, creating the kind of rotational motion needed to power the wheels of an EV. Modern electric motors have replaced the brushes described here with sensors and solid-state switches.

Of course, electric motors cannot run without a source of electricity. In EVs, that source is usually a chemical battery. All atoms, including those that make up batteries, contain three major particles. Positively charged protons and charge-free neutrons are found in the center of the atom, called its nucleus. Electrons, which are negatively charged, circle the nucleus in a

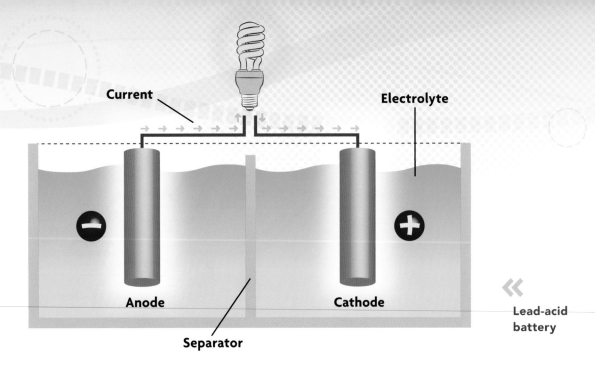

Current

Electrolyte

Anode

Cathode

Separator

Lead-acid battery

cloud. Electricity is the flow of electrons from one atom to another, and batteries are a way of harnessing that flow.

A battery has four key components: an anode, a cathode, a separator, and an electrolyte. The anode and cathode are both classified as electrodes, or conductors that provide electric contact. The anode is a negative electrode that contains a high concentration of electrons. The cathode is a positively charged electrode that contains a high concentration of protons. The separator keeps the electrodes from touching. These three layers are surrounded by an electrolyte, or solution that conducts electricity, which can be liquid or solid. The electrolyte reacts with the poles to initiate an electron imbalance necessary to produce electricity.

Current is the flow of electrons from the anode to the cathode. They can't move between the two directly, however, because of the separator. Instead, the electrons travel out of the anode, down a wire, and pass through whatever device needs power. Once they exit the device—in the case of EVs, the electric motor—the electrons reach the cathode. The more electrons there are flowing, the stronger the current will be. Batteries create direct current, meaning the electrons flow in only one direction. With alternating current, like that provided by your wall sockets, the electrons change direction at a fixed rate.

The first batteries were invented in 1860 and used a chemistry called lead-acid, using sheets of pure lead as the cathode and anode; these sheets were dipped in weak sulfuric acid to act as the electrolyte. Lead-acid batteries have not changed much since then. Their anodes are still made of pure lead, while their cathodes are usually lead dioxide. These batteries are cheap and tough, but they have a disadvantage: low energy density. Relative to the weight of the battery, they do not produce a lot of power.

Despite this, most EVs used lead-acid batteries until the 1990s. At that point, carmakers upgraded to nickel metal hydride (NiMH). These NiMH batteries offer similar safety and durability, but have higher energy density.

BATTERY PRAISE AND PERIL

Batteries received much praise when they were first invented. As an article in the June 11, 1881, edition of the *New York Times* put it, "It is quite possible that the man who has taught us to put up electricity in bottles has accomplished greater things than any inventor who has yet appeared."[3]

Although their invention was revolutionary, early batteries were not perfect. Water had to be added to keep the electrolyte at the proper level, which could be a difficult task. Automaker Charles Duryea once said, "A set of batteries [is] worse to take care of than a hospital full of sick dogs."[4]

When a driver turns the key of an electric vehicle, it activates a starter switch, which sends electricity from the battery to the controller. The controller determines how much energy goes to the motor based on the signals coming from the driver's pedals. More pressure on the pedal means more electricity goes to the motor, creating more speed.

REINVENTING THE EV

For more than 100 years, electric vehicle researchers have been looking for ways to squeeze more miles out of every battery charge. Building with lighter materials helps, as does decreasing rolling resistance.

Increasing range also involves minimizing aerodynamic drag, a force that resists the motion of the vehicle as it travels through the air. Drag is caused by friction between air molecules and the exterior surface of the car, and can be reduced by using smooth, slippery body panels.

The shape of the vehicle also has a huge impact. In fact, engineers at GM tested their electric Chevrolet Volt in a wind tunnel for more than 700 hours, studying how the wind hit the car and trying to optimize its body shape.[5]

Something called regenerative braking also plays a role in EV efficiency. When the driver of a gas-powered car hits the brakes, pads press against the wheels to slow their rotation. The kinetic energy, or movement, that was moving the car forward is converted to friction, and lost as heat. When the driver of an electric-powered car hits the brakes, however, the electric motor actually goes into reverse. The forward movement of the car is counteracted by the torque, or turning force, created during this reversal. When the motor reverses, it also becomes a generator, converting the captured movement back into electricity to store in the car's battery. This energy capture method is called regenerative braking.

Regenerative braking is believed to have been invented by M. A. Darracq in 1897. It reclaims approximately 30 percent of the energy that a gas-powered car loses as heat.[6] Although this technology conserves energy, it can be less efficient at bringing a car to a quick stop. Therefore, most electric vehicles also have backup friction brakes, which can be necessary in situations where quick, powerful braking is necessary.

While regenerative braking conserves energy under normal driving conditions, coasting, or moving on momentum, is even better. The most energy-efficient cars greatly reduce their energy use by utilizing coasting.

FILLING THE TANK

No matter how efficient an EV is, its batteries will eventually run down. This is due to decreasing electric pressure, or voltage. In a battery, voltage is created by the attraction of the electrons in the anode to the protons in the cathode. The bigger the difference is between those positive and negative charges, the higher the voltage will be. As an EV draws current from the battery, however, electrons migrate from the anode to the cathode, and the charges at the two electrodes start to balance out. The battery has to be recharged—that is, the electrons have to be sent back to the anode—before the car will drive any further.

EV batteries are charged by being plugged into an electricity source in one of two ways. Inductive charging takes advantage of the relationship between magnetism and electricity. Current methods use a paddle that fits into a socket on the vehicle, creating a magnetic coupling where a change in current creates voltage. This is very safe and easy for owners, but requires a special, external charging station. Wireless inductive charging concept cars were also being developed as of 2012. The concept is that a wireless inductive charger is embedded into a ground pad, and the driver parks above it to charge.

Conductive charging, which uses a special cord with a regular plug and wall socket, is the most common charging method. It's also a little controversial because approximately 50 percent of the electricity that's made in the United States comes from power plants that burn coal, a fossil fuel.[7] This means that many electric cars cannot be charged without being responsible for the production of fossil fuel emissions.

These facts have caused people to question whether common conductive-charged EVs are actually any greener than ICEs. As Bill Reinert of Toyota USA put it, "You don't end up with a better environmental performance, you end up with a longer tailpipe."[8]

Others argue, however, that EVs that are charged with electricity that was created by burning coal are still greener than gas-powered vehicles. One reason for this belief is that unlike cars, electric power plants tend to be in rural areas farther away from large numbers of people, which reduces the health impact of emissions. Another is that there are stricter standards governing emissions from power plants than those released from cars. On the other hand, because demand for electricity is increasing, carbon dioxide emissions are also expected to increase.

In order to minimize emissions, the best way to charge an EV is with renewable electricity. One option is hydroelectric power, or renewable water power. Car batteries can be charged using wind power as well. It's estimated that wind turbines placed in the American Midwest could replace 30 percent of the energy currently produced by coal-burning power plants.[9] Solar power is another source of renewable energy. Some drivers are already using electricity produced by home solar panels to charge their electric cars.

TECHNOLOGICAL LIMITATIONS

It will likely take more than a decade for car manufacturers and consumers to make the change to another fuel source and engine form. This is why the insight and technology to move toward wider use of electric vehicles must be developed today if we are to have electricity-powered cars in the near future. Batteries are still expensive, so electric vehicles are still more expensive than gas-powered options. Batteries are also still sensitive to temperature: they tend to lose voltage when it's cold outside, and using the car's heating system can drain the battery significantly. So can the extra weight of passengers or cargo or driving up hills. Managing and maintaining an EV can be complex because of the need to carefully monitor and integrate the batteries' condition and health as well as the demands of the driver.

Unlike a gas tank, which can be filled in minutes, EV batteries still take between four and ten hours to fully recharge. Battery range can vary greatly depending on driving habits, such as speed, terrain, and use of other vehicle systems including the heat or air conditioning. Range estimates before recharging an EV battery are anywhere from 75 to 200 miles (120 to 322 km), and needing hours to recharge is a serious issue on longer journeys because charging stations are still hard to find.

Researchers continue innovating hybrid vehicles. The concept of combining the best features of two power sources while avoiding their drawbacks remains an inspiration.

REDUCE, REUSE, RECYCLE

Batteries can only be charged so many times before they have to be replaced. Approximately 98 percent of "dead" lead-acid batteries get recycled.[10] The sulfuric acid is either reused or neutralized and discarded. The electrodes are melted and remade into new batteries. Even the plastic casings are cleaned, broken down, and reused.

CHAPTER 5

HYBRIDS

The term *hybrid*, as applied to vehicles, describes something with two distinct components performing a similar function. Hybrid vehicles are any vehicles that have two power sources. The first power source is typically electricity, with the most common second source being gasoline. However, vehicles are now also being developed that use a combination of hydrogen and electricity or of compressed air and diesel fuel. As of 2012, gasoline hybrid electric vehicles (HEVs) were the most common hybrids. Hybrid technology allows engineers to combine the high power and energy density of fossil fuels with the high efficiency of an electric motor as the second energy source. This creates cars with several advantages over other types of vehicles.

HEV batteries are smaller than those used in EVs, which makes these cars more affordable than their all-electric counterparts. HEVs also have the ability to refuel at

≪ **Many established car models, even SUVs such as the Ford Escape, are being made available as hybrids.**

FOUNDER OF THE MODERN HYBRID

Dr. Victor Wouk became interested in alternative vehicles in 1962 when he was asked to test a battery-powered car. He felt that pure EVs were impractical but loved the idea of hybrids. During the early 1970s, Wouk received a grant from the EPA to create a hybrid using a 1972 Buick Skylark.

Wouk's prototype had a top speed of 85 miles per hour (137 km/h) and met the strictest emissions standards of the day. It also got 30 miles per gallon (13 km/L)[1]. This is more than modern Buick HEV miles per gallon. But the project lost its funding and Wouk's design was never mass-produced. Despite this, he's still known as the founder of the modern hybrid car movement.

any gas station and use gasoline power, so they never suffer the range problems that can be an issue with electric cars.

All other factors being equal, by combining power sources, HEVs can travel farther on one tank of gasoline than an ICE-only vehicle while producing fewer tailpipe emissions. Although HEVs do use gasoline, their emissions are lower because they run in electric mode part of the time.

SERIES HYBRIDS

There are two ways to construct an HEV: in series or in parallel. Series hybrids run the most simply. In series hybrids the ICE converts the chemical energy of gasoline into mechanical energy. This mechanical energy is then fed through a generator, creating electricity. The electricity powers the electric motor, which turns the vehicle's wheels. In parallel hybrids, on the other hand, both the ICE and the electric motor can move the wheels.

In simple terms, a series hybrid is an EV that uses an ICE to achieve extra range. Except during hill climbing and fast acceleration, most ICE vehicles need only a small fraction of the total power their engines produce, and the remaining power is often unused. But because they are not directly connected, series hybrid ICEs can always run at their most efficient torque and speed without having to take the vehicle's speed and motion into consideration. One drawback of this design, however, is that because the ICE is the vehicle's sole source of energy, it must be big enough to handle the worst possible driving conditions the vehicle could ever encounter, and therefore must be the same size or even bigger than the ICEs in purely gasoline-powered cars. Because the electric motor is the sole source of motion, it also has to be full-sized. Because of these large motors, series hybrids are expensive to produce and have a lower fuel economy than parallel hybrids, meaning they also cost more to drive.

PARALLEL HYBRIDS

A parallel hybrid is an ICE-powered vehicle that is assisted by an electric motor. In vehicles that make use of parallel design, both the engine and the electric motor can move the wheels. Or, when extra power is needed for hills, acceleration, and higher speeds, the engine and the motor

SERIES HYBRID

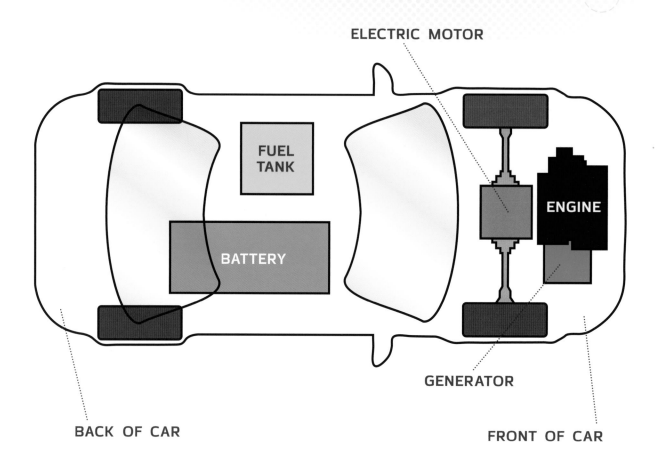

ELECTRIC MOTOR

FUEL TANK

ENGINE

BATTERY

GENERATOR

BACK OF CAR

FRONT OF CAR

PARALLEL HYBRID

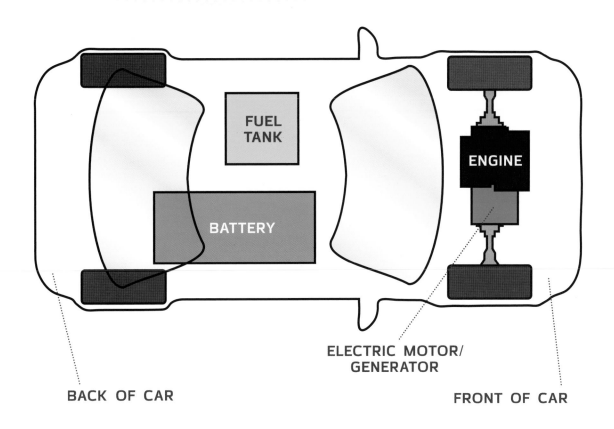

FUEL
TANK

ENGINE

BATTERY

ELECTRIC MOTOR/
GENERATOR

BACK OF CAR

FRONT OF CAR

THE LOHNER-PORSCHE HYBRID ELECTRIC VEHICLE

Although he wasn't the first inventor to tinker with hybrids, Dr. Ferdinand Porsche (1875–1952) is recognized for his innovative designs. Porsche built his first hybrid in 1902 while working for Lohner's Electric Vehicle Company. It was a series model with a 20-horsepower, four-cylinder engine and a 21-kilowatt generator. The generator powered motors in the front wheel hubs and charged lead-acid batteries. When running on battery power alone, the car had a range of 40 miles (64 km).[2]

However, like many automakers of the time, Porsche eventually decided hybrids were too expensive to mass-produce. This is why he switched to the gasoline-powered vehicles that bear his name today.

can do the work together. Since neither the ICE nor the electric motor need to do all the work, parallel hybrids can have smaller components than series HEVs, making them less expensive while achieving the same or better performance.

The most well-known parallel hybrid is the Toyota Prius, the first HEV to be mass-produced by a major automobile manufacturer. The Prius starts moving using only its electric motor, while the gas engine kicks in at higher speeds. The engine also turns off when the car is stopped in traffic, saving the fuel that is normally burned by ICE cars while they idle.

When the Prius's combustion engine produces more energy than is needed for driving, the excess charges the car's batteries. The batteries also charge when the Prius goes

downhill, as well as during regenerative braking. Toyota says up to 20 percent of the vehicle's power comes from these energy-capture methods.[3] Altogether, the Prius models are the most efficient economy and midsize vehicles currently available compared to ICE vehicles and other hybrids; they also produce 70 percent fewer emissions.[4]

CHALLENGES AND COMPARISONS

Compared to gasoline-powered cars, hybrids have many advantages. But they are still not perfect. First, they are more complicated than other vehicles, making them more difficult to repair. Their complexity can also make them more difficult to manage and maintain due to the need to manage and optimize two power sources operating at the same time. Another disadvantage of hybrids is that the cost of the battery makes them more expensive to purchase than ICE vehicles. In the past, the cost of battery replacement also had to be considered, as no battery can be recharged indefinitely. However, the batteries used in most of today's hybrids have been designed to last for the life of the car, making this issue obsolete. Recent

GAS CARS VERSUS HYBRIDS[5]

	2012 Toyota Camry [ICE]	2012 Camry Hybrid [HEV]	2012 Ford Fusion [ICE]	2012 Fusion Hybrid [HEV]	2012 Buick Regal [ICE]	2012 Regal Hybrid [HEV]
Miles per gallon	28	41	25	39	23	29
Cost per 25 miles	3.00	2.05	3.36	2.15	3.65	2.90
Barrels of oil per year	11.8	8.0	13.2	8.4	14.3	11.4
Tailpipe CO_2 (grams per mile)	317	217	355	228	386	306
Miles per tank of gasoline	428 (17-gallon tank)	627 (17-gallon tank)	394 (S FWD model: 17.5-gallon tank)	614 (17.5-gallon tank)	373 (18-gallon tank)	Unknown (18-gallon tank)

data provided by Toyota has proved this to be the case, and newer batteries hitting the current market are even better.

Hybrid batteries have both advantages and disadvantages compared to their counterparts used in EVs. HEV batteries are a little different than those used in pure EVs: they store less energy, but they create more power. Since hybrid vehicles have ICEs to assist them, they do not need to store as much energy, which is an advantage. On the other hand, HEVs can provide quicker acceleration, which requires batteries with greater strength, and these can be more expensive.

Another disadvantage to hybrids in comparison to EVs is that HEVs create tailpipe emissions due to their gasoline-powered ICEs. One way to reduce these emissions is by combining an electric motor with a diesel-powered ICE engine, which emits less carbon than gasoline-powered ICEs, or a flex-fuel engine, which can use alternative fuels such as ethanol. Ford's Escape hybrid is an example of a vehicle that does just that. Another approach is combining the best features of a hybrid with the best features of an EV to create plug-in HEVs, which have batteries that can be charged using household electricity. Many car designers feel HEVs hold great promise for the future of cleaner, greener transportation.

PLUG-IN HYBRID ELECTRIC VEHICLES

Plug-in hybrid electric vehicles (PHEVs) combine the best aspect of EVs (the grid-rechargeable battery) and the best aspect of hybrids (implementing two power sources) for added efficiency and power. Like regular HEVs, PHEVs combine electric power with power from a second source, typically an ICE. However, PHEVs differ from HEVs in one critical way. As well as charging from the car's onboard generator, PHEV batteries can also be charged by plugging them into the electric grid, using electricity from an owner's home or work. In this way, PHEVs are similar to EVs, which can also plug in and charge from the electric grid. However, a PHEV is different from an EV because it has a second power component, just as regular hybrids do. Due to this second power component, PHEVs do not have to be charged at high power, or high voltage. Both EVs and PHEVs can use electricity from ordinary household plugs, but

 PHEVs can be recharged using a regular electric wall socket.

EVs require special cords that provide high power, while PHEVs can use ordinary plugs and cords. This greatly reduces the costs of the charging infrastructure.

Being able to charge the batteries from the grid allows PHEV designers to increase the battery size, which also increases the distance such vehicles can travel using electric power alone. This is known as the vehicle's all-electric range. PHEVs' electric ranges are labeled: a car labeled PHEV55, for example, has an all-electric range of 55 miles (89 km).

THE POWER OF THE PLUG

Andrew Frank is a professor of engineering at the University of California Davis who specializes in advanced vehicle technology. In 1972, Frank and his students improved on Porsche's designs to build the first modern PHEV. During the early 1990s, Frank's team was able to achieve 3,300 miles per gallon (1,403 km/L) by putting a lawn mower engine in a vehicle using kinetic energy storage.[1]

Frank doesn't believe you have to sacrifice performance to achieve energy efficiency. His minimum goal is 100 miles per gallon (43 km/L) in cars that can go from 0 to 60 miles per hour (0 to 97 km/h) in less than ten seconds. As Frank said in 2006, "We had converted a Ford Explorer [an ICE vehicle] into a plug-in hybrid, and it had so much torque that we couldn't keep the axles from snapping. With six of my students in there, it could still burn rubber."[2] This was no small accomplishment, as many critics still believe hybrid vehicles sacrifice performance for efficiency.

One invention of Frank's that helped make these results possible is called the continuously variable transmission (CVT). Its function is to blend the power of a hybrid's engine and motor into a single drivetrain, or the parts that connect the transmission to the drive axles. An ICE vehicle with an automatic transmission has 700 moving parts, but Frank's design uses only 12. Fewer moving parts equals more efficiency and lower costs.

COMPUTER CONTROLS

Drivers today are used to the controls in a traditional ICE vehicle: that is, an accelerator, a brake pedal, and a shifter that provides park,

FINDING THE RIGHT DESIGN

In 2009, Andy Frank's team used ADVISOR (software designed by engineers at the National Renewable Energy Laboratory and the US Department of Energy) to test power sources for step vans—the kind FedEx uses to deliver packages, for example. ADVISOR is a research tool that allows scientists to virtually design and test a vehicle completely without taking the time and expense to build it in the real world.

Frank's group tested gasoline vans, series HEVs, and both regular and plug-in parallel HEVs. In every test, the plug-in parallel hybrid had the best fuel economy: in one case, the HEV was 168.3 percent better than the manual-transmission ICE van! The same PHEV could reach 60 miles per hour (97 km/h) in 25.7 seconds, while the gas-powered van needed 38.2 seconds to do the same thing.[3]

reverse, neutral, drive, and low gear modes. The PHEV, however, has many other modes, which makes it more complex to drive. HEV modes have to be automated by some sort of controls in order to be easily integrated for consumer use. To bring the PHEV into the consumer marketplace, the vehicle's additional complexity had to become computer controlled. Advances in modern PHEVs have introduced sophisticated computers that control their energy use during driving. The computer switches the car among several different modes depending on the amount of energy left in the battery. The cars Frank designed and constructed to demonstrate the PHEV concept from 1990 to 2010 all featured computer controls that manage all the various modes of operation. The main modes are:

> All-electric—As in an EV, this is a mode in which the only source of energy is the battery.

> Charge-depleting—A mode in which at least some of the energy comes from the battery (the gasoline engine may be working as well).

> Charge-sustaining—The gasoline engine provides all of the driving energy in this mode, while maintaining the battery's state of charge within a certain range (HEVs operate in this mode most of the time).

> Engine-only mode—The car operates like a conventional ICE vehicle in this mode.

 PHEVs have many computer controls and displays, which can make owning and operating them more complex.

To take full advantage of their larger batteries, PHEVs usually run in all-electric mode, then switch to charge-sustaining mode when the battery gets too weak to power the vehicle. The Chevrolet Volt has a mode that does this.

Scientists are currently working to develop new control software for hybrids and plug-ins. Their goal is to optimize both energy management (the vehicle's efficiency and emissions) and drivability (the vehicle's performance, comfort, and safety). It is a challenging problem, because real-world driving conditions are complex and variable. Additionally, aggressive driving—with rapid acceleration and high speeds—uses more energy than conservative driving, no matter the vehicle type. A 2010 study in the United Kingdom found that when different people took the same car around a test track, aggressive drivers used up to twice as much energy.[4]

Innovative computer control programs also include research and ideas from many different scientific fields to create vehicles that can provide the right mix of power for any situation. These fields include genetics, neurobiology, and game theory. For example, in some vehicles, the computer controller is rewarded with better fuel economy when it provides the right power mix for the driver's demands. These types of controllers are the most successful because they (the controller) actually learn as the vehicle is driven.

V2G

Another exciting possibility for PHEVs is known as vehicle to grid power, or V2G. Unlike inductive, magnetic charging systems, which allow energy to flow in only one direction (from the charger to the car), the conductive (wall socket) chargers used by some PHEVs can be bi-directional. This would mean that electricity stored in a PHEV's battery could potentially be sent back into the electric grid. It is even possible that electricity companies might someday pay a vehicle's owner in exchange for the V2G power. For now, V2G power is only theoretical, but research continues into this exciting possibility.

PHEV VERSUS HEV, EV, AND ICEV

PHEVs offer several advantages over EVs, HEVs, and ICEVs. PHEVs are cheaper to drive than ICEs because as of 2012, electricity is less expensive than gasoline.[5] The alternative vehicles that do use gasoline use less than conventional ICE vehicles. PHEVs also use less gas than HEVs because their batteries are larger, extending their all-electric range. As a result of using less gasoline, PHEVs decrease nitrogen oxide emissions by 25 to 55 percent relative to HEVs, and they also decrease greenhouse gas emissions by 35 to 65 percent.[6]

With their many advantages, many critics feel PHEVs are a clear choice for greening transportation throughout the world. The only way to really understand any vehicle's impact on the environment is to look at *all* the emissions it produces, however, not just those coming directly from a tailpipe. That includes emissions produced during:

> the mining or extraction of non-renewable resources (gas, coal, oil) or the manufacturing of other liquid fuel (such as biofuels)

PHEVS OUT-GREEN EVS

In addition to using well-to-wheels calculations, which take fuel production and distribution effects into consideration, alternative vehicles can be compared by how many miles they can electrify, or drive without using gasoline. For example, an EV10 can electrify any trip that lasts up to 10 miles (16 km), its maximum range. So can a PHEV10. The PHEV can also electrify the first 10 miles of trips that cover longer distances by driving in gasoline hybrid mode after the batteries run down to a minimum. PHEV10s could therefore be considered superior to EV10s because they electrify more overall miles. The Chevrolet Volt has a 35-mile (56 km) all-electric range. Volt drivers drive electrically approximately 60 percent of the time.[7]

- production of the fuel (refining the oil or generating the electricity) that will charge the battery

- transportation and distribution (getting the fuel to the gas station or the electricity into the electric grid)

- the vehicle's refueling process, and

- any processing or conversions that happen in the vehicle itself.

Because this type of research looks at every stage of the process, from fuel extraction to use in the vehicle, it's known as well-to-wheels analysis. The results of these tests vary depending on the kind of electricity used to charge a PHEV's batteries. If a PHEV uses fossil fuels and gets its charge from electricity sourced from fossil fuels, it is not green. A PHEV is only as green as the electricity source that powers it. Thus, if a PHEV's battery is charged only with solar or wind energy and its liquid fuel energy comes from bio-sources such as ethanol, a PHEV can be certified as a zero emissions vehicle.

PHEV'S ROAD AHEAD

In his State of the Union address in 2011, President Obama restated the official goal he set in 2008 to have 1 million PHEVs on the road by 2015. Frank says that until recent years, this would not have been possible because "there were missing links that really made the concept difficult."[8] But some of these missing innovations have now been created. One was Frank's own continuously variable transmission. Another missing component that has now been developed is the sophisticated computers that control a PHEV's power flow. A third component is improved battery efficiency, energy, and high costs—something scientists are still working on. In 2012, President Obama created the Blueprint for a Secure Energy Future, which aims to improve clean energy standards and increase renewable energy use. The availability of more clean energy sources would increase the probability of PHEVs using a green source for power.

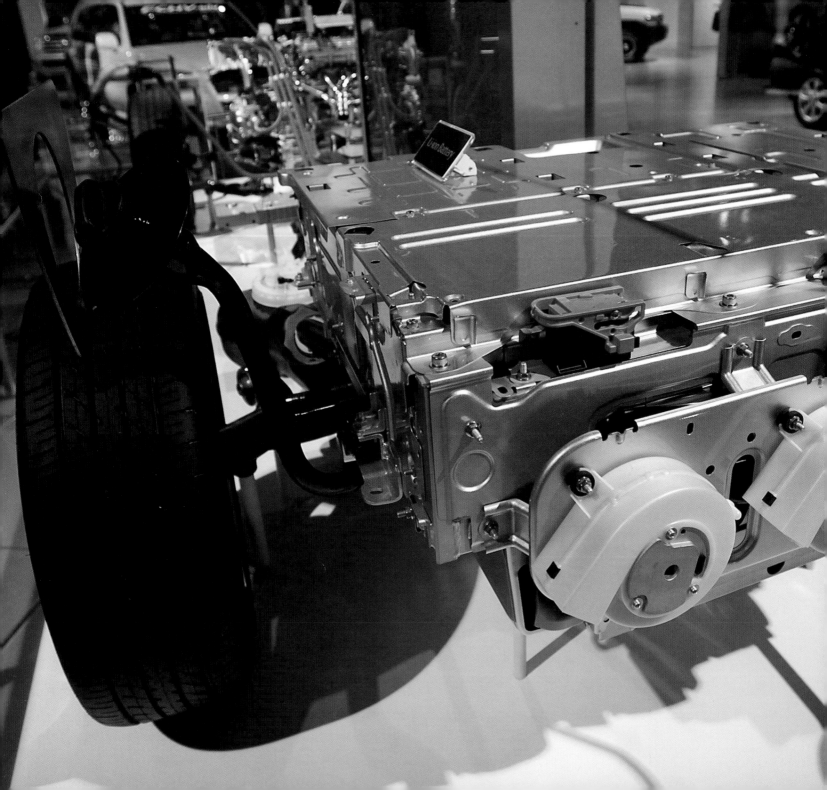

CHAPTER 7

LITHIUM BATTERIES: PROMISE AND PERIL

All alternative vehicles need safe, reasonably priced batteries that last as long as the vehicle and work under a wide range of weather conditions. They have to pack maximum power into the smallest possible volume and weight. The energy capacity needs to be substantial enough to provide a desirable driving range for consumers. However, providing the energy necessary to travel greater distances translates to a bigger battery, adding weight that works against efficiency.

Finding a battery powerful enough to compete with or surpass ICE capabilities remains a challenge. The problem has been recognized for more than a century. "What is required to meet motor carriage conditions," said Andrew Riker in 1897, "is a battery capable of very heavy discharges but still not of excessive weight, and this requires some special type of battery."[1] Carmakers began using nickel metal hydride (NiMH)

« **Many researchers are looking to lithium-ion batteries as a possible solution for lightweight, powerful batteries for alternative vehicles.**

batteries, which have higher energy density, over heavy lead-acid batteries during the late 1980s. But there was still room for improvement.

When Martin Eberhard cofounded Tesla Motors in 2003, his goal was to build "the hottest electric cars the world has ever seen." It seemed like the only way to do so would be to use the powerful, compact new batteries that made portable cell phones possible. "Lithium-ion batteries were at the top of my mind," Eberhard says, "because in my rough calculations, you could actually fit enough batteries into a car to make a meaningful car."[2]

FROM LEAD TO LITHIUM

Lithium is a metal that has half the density of water and is more than 30 times lighter than lead, the metal used in typical batteries. Lithium has both high specific energy and high energy density.

THE TESLA ROADSTER

Tesla's all-electric Roadster can travel up to 245 miles (394 km) per charge and accelerates from 0 to 60 miles per hour (0 to 96 km/h) in only 3.7 seconds. These achievements are possible due to their Li-ION batteries, which have the highest energy density in the industry. The Roadster's battery pack contains 6,831 cells and weighs 990 pounds (449 kg). It uses a liquid cooling system to keep the batteries from overheating, but comes with a battery warmer so the car can be charged during periods of cold temperatures. Perhaps best of all, the Roadster's batteries are nontoxic and 60 percent recyclable.[3]

There are also downsides, however. The Tesla Roadster is expensive, with a base price of more than $100,000, and it takes up to 3.5 hours to charge using a wall plug-in.

In 1907, Thomas Edison filed a patent for what might have been the very first lithium battery. According to his application, adding 0.07 ounces (2 g) of lithium hydroxide to every 3.4 fluid ounces (100 mL) of electrolyte increased a battery's capacity by 10 percent and remarkably extended the amount of time it could hold a charge.[4] Another key breakthrough came 80 years later when Keizaburo Tozawa, head of battery company Sony Eveready, created a lithium-ion (Li-ION) battery with voltage, or potential electric energy, three times higher than the NiMH batteries being used most commonly at the time.[5]

Li-ION batteries have better charging performance than NiMH batteries and their chemistry is easier to recycle. It was not long before they were being used to power EVs. But Li-ION batteries have two major drawbacks. First, they are expensive to make. Worse yet, they can also be dangerous.

BATTERIES CATCHING FIRE

A basic Li-ION battery has a carbon-lithium anode and a cathode combining lithium, oxygen, and a metal such as cobalt. If the battery overheats during use or recharging, elemental lithium, which can react violently with water and oxygen, can be produced. This is a problem because overheating also causes the cathodes to release oxygen gas. The resulting reaction can cause lithium batteries to catch fire.

ARE BATTERIES MORE SECURE THAN OIL?

Most of the world's lithium comes from Bolivia, Chile, and Argentina. This concentration of resources has led to concern about potential energy security should plug-ins and EVs eventually replace gasoline-powered cars. As Henry Ford's great-grandson, William Clay Ford Jr., put it in 2008, "We really don't want to trade one foreign dependency—oil—for another foreign dependency—batteries."[6]

But Seth Fletcher, author of *Bottled Lighting*, doesn't really see it that way. "After all," he says, "imported batteries are not like imported oil. An advanced auto battery is a piece of high technology designed to last for years. Oil is a commodity we buy millions of barrels of each day and then burn for fuel."[7]

Around the year 2005, videos of flaming Li-ION laptop batteries began circulating online, creating concern. Because vehicle batteries typically weigh hundreds of pounds, a lithium car battery catching fire would be incredibly dangerous. For this reason, scientists are searching for breakthrough lithium chemistries that balance the incredible power of this technology with the necessary safety.

When designing a lithium battery for the Chevrolet Volt, a PHEV, General Motors looked for a battery that:

> could provide a 40-mile (64 km) all-electric range with acceleration from 0 to 60 miles per hour (0 to 97 km/h) in eight seconds

> could withstand 5,000 full discharges without losing more than 10 percent of its capacity

A Chevy Volt being manufactured in early October 2011

> could fit in the space available and weighed no more than 400 pounds (181 kg).[8]

There was one more requirement: the battery had to be safe. In June 2011, it was reported to the National Highway Traffic Safety Administration (NHTSA) that fire occurred at the MGA Research test facility in Wisconsin, where a Chevrolet Volt was crash-tested three weeks prior, on May 12. According to the NHTSA, which collaborated with a battery expert, the fire was started by the crash-tested Volt. The NHTSA report revealed that the car's battery had been damaged and the liquid cooling system ruptured.[9] The coolant leaked and the battery started on fire. Safety standards for lithium batteries require them to be fully discharged following an accident, and it was revealed that procedure was not followed in this case.

Although no roadside incidents involving a Volt catching fire had been reported, the NHTSA launched a defect investigation that November. In return, GM suggested modifications to the Volt in December. A stronger structure guarding the battery from damage in the event of a crash, and a sensor observing battery coolant levels were incorporated in future Volts, and to thousands that had already been sold.

Bob Lutz has worked for General Motors and is one of the Volt's biggest supporters. He says no Volt has ever exploded under real world conditions, whereas "250,000 conventional gasoline-powered cars catch fire every year in the US."[10] Aaron Bragman, who has 20 years of experience in the automotive industry but has never worked for GM, agrees: "There's very little threat to anyone from these vehicles," he says. "There is more of a threat involved in carting

FLAMING FAILURES

During the 1970s, Michael Stanley Whittingham and his team at oil and gas giant Exxon Mobil Corporation were working to develop one of the first rechargeable lithium batteries. The experiments were so dangerous that the local fire department eventually threatened to charge Exxon for the special chemicals needed to put out the many fires the team accidentally started. Ultimately, however, the team was successful. Their lithium batteries were first used to power watches, but even from the beginning, Exxon was planning to use them in electric vehicles. Prototype cars were made, but the project was cut due to the recession of the 1980s.

around 15 gallons of highly flammable liquid [gasoline]."[11] Some people, however, continue to express concerns.

LITHIUM TIN WHISKERS

Anodes made of lithium and tin have a higher specific energy than traditional carbon-lithium anodes. Unfortunately, when lithium rebonds with tin during recharging, the compound expands by 260 percent. This puts a great deal of physical stress on the anode, and this stress expresses itself in the form of microscopic crystals called tin whiskers.

In one test, approximately 1,300 whiskers formed on every square millimeter of the anode's surface.[12] After several discharge/recharge cycles, the anode disintegrated, destroying the battery's capacity. Even if an anode can remain intact after tin whiskers have formed, tin whiskers can grow long enough to penetrate the separator between the electrodes, shorting out the battery and causing the whole system to fail.

Yi Cui, a professor at Stanford University, is the head of a research group searching for ways to beat tin whiskers. They are using lithium-silicone anodes, which expand by as much as 400 percent during cycling; this expansion can stress the anode and create whiskers.

However, the secret to Cui's approach is nanotechnology. The anode his team has constructed is basically *made* of whiskers, so they cannot fracture any further. "If the object is already smaller than the smallest thing you can break, they don't break any more," said Dr. Cui.[13] He was right. In lab tests, nanowire batteries have high energy levels and hold their capacity over time.

Researchers continue working on creating safer, more efficient batteries for alternative vehicles. As battery challenges persist, many car designers are considering another device that is similar, but not identical, to a battery: the fuel cell.

« **A NASA engineer examines tin whiskers that have sprouted on an electric device.**

CHAPTER 8

FUEL CELL VEHICLES

I magine an energy source that lasts longer than batteries and contains no toxic chemicals. It would be plentiful, safe, and have a higher energy per mass than any other fuel on earth. A vehicle that used it could be refueled as easily as a gasoline-powered car, but it would produce only one emission—water pure enough to drink.

Such an energy source is not mere science fiction. It's hydrogen gas. And when it's piped into a fuel cell, it's a potent source of electricity. That electricity can be used to power an electric motor, creating a series hybrid called a fuel cell vehicle (FCV) that is twice as efficient as an ICE vehicle.[1]

INSIDE A FUEL CELL

A hydrogen fuel cell is a lot like a battery that is refueled instead of being recharged. Hydrogen gas is pumped into the cell at the anode. Each molecule of hydrogen then

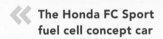

The Honda FC Sport fuel cell concept car

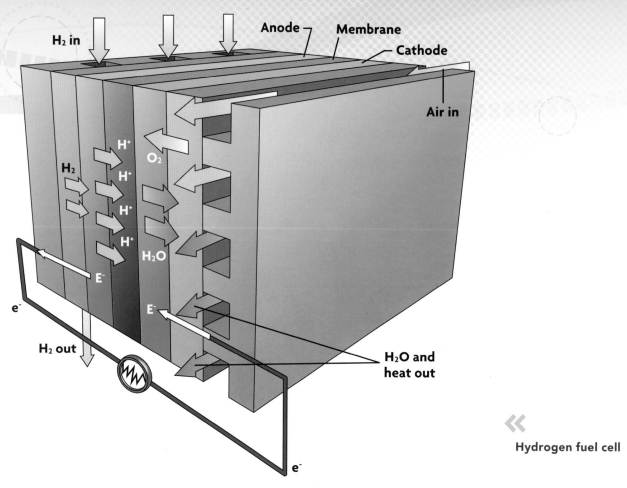

H₂ in

Anode — **Membrane** — **Cathode**

Air in

H⁺
H₂   O₂
H⁺

H⁺

H⁺
H₂O

E⁻

E⁻

e⁻

H₂ out

H₂O and heat out

e⁻

«

Hydrogen fuel cell

splits into an electron and a proton. The electrons flow through an external circuit, creating electricity. The protons pass through a proton exchange membrane to the cathode, where they combine with electrons and oxygen from the air, creating water and heat. This is why hydrogen fuel cells produce water, heat, and electricity but no pollution.

There are some drawbacks to this fuel source, however. One hydrogen fuel cell produces less than one volt of energy, which is why many fuel cells have to be combined to create larger fuel stacks. Other disadvantages are that the chemical reaction that powers these cells takes place only at high temperatures—up to 1,800 degrees Fahrenheit (1,000°C). Additionally, electricity production does not begin immediately; instead, it requires start up time, which can be anywhere from a few seconds to several minutes, depending on the design.

The first hydrogen fuel cells were invented in 1839 by Welsh scientist Sir William Grove. But fuel cells did not become practical as a power source until 1959, when Francis Bacon designed one with a power output of five kilowatts. His design was the only major fuel cell innovation in more than 100 years, and NASA used it beginning in the 1960s to send the Apollo space rocket and its astronauts into space. The NASA space program continued to use light and powerful liquid hydrogen for more than 50 years.

HYDROGEN

Hydrogen is the most abundant element in the universe. However, hydrogen gas is not found on its own in nature, but instead is always fused with another element. Therefore hydrogen itself is not an energy source, although it does contain energy in and of itself. Instead, it's considered an energy carrier, or fuel. Pure hydrogen must be produced by splitting it from other entities, such as water or fossil fuels, which can often be a disadvantage because these production methods are not always green.

There are two methods that are used most often to produce hydrogen. One is called reforming, a process that extracts hydrogen gas from the hydrocarbons in fossil fuels. The fossil fuels that can be used in this method include ethanol, propane, gasoline, and natural gas. The cheapest and most common method of making hydrogen uses natural gas. A main component of natural gas is methane, a molecule that reacts with steam to produce hydrogen, carbon monoxide, and carbon dioxide. In the United States, approximately 95 percent of the hydrogen produced is extracted from natural gas.[2]

Regardless of which fossil fuel is used, hydrogen reforming produces carbon dioxide. This means that even though hydrogen fuel cells do not produce pollutants, the means of creating the hydrogen needed to power the fuel cells does. However, hydrogen production produces less carbon dioxide than ICEs do.

ELECTROLYSIS

The simplest and most efficient method of producing hydrogen is called electrolysis. Using this technique, electricity is pumped through water, producing oxygen and hydrogen gases. The hydrogen can then be fed through a fuel cell, which reverses the reaction, producing electricity and water.

The downside of using electrolysis to obtain hydrogen is how much electricity is used in the process. Professor Frank and Ulf Bossel, the founder of the European Fuel Cell Forum, agree that an FCV uses four times as much electricity per mile as a similarly sized EV.[3] And that means four times as many emissions are created by the production of that electricity.

In other words, electrolysis will only be a workable alternative to the pollution created by hydrogen production via fossil fuel reforming when clean, renewable electricity—as from solar or wind power—can be cheaply and abundantly produced.

BALLARD FUEL CELLS

One of the most advanced fuel cells made today was developed by Canadian company Ballard Power Corporation. Ballard fuel cells are compact, use direct electrolysis, and begin producing electricity relatively quickly. They also work at the comparatively low temperature of 176 degrees Fahrenheit (80°C).[4] On August 16, 2007, Ford's Fusion 999, which uses Ballard fuel cells, set a land speed record of 207.297 miles per hour (333.61 km/h).[5] Ballard cells use expensive platinum catalysts, however, and if their proton exchange membranes dry out or become contaminated by heavy metal ions, failure of the fuel cell occurs.

HYDROGEN AND THE HINDENBURG

In 1937 the Hindenburg—a hydrogen-filled airship—caught on fire and was completely destroyed. This is one reason why many people believe hydrogen is too dangerous to be used in vehicles. However, recent research shows the Hindenburg disaster was actually caused by the flammable fabric that surrounded the hydrogen, not the hydrogen itself.

STORAGE AND COST

There are two additional barriers to using hydrogen as an energy source: storage and cost. Because liquid hydrogen turns to a gas at temperatures higher than minus 423 degrees Fahrenheit (-253°C), it is almost impossible to store as a liquid. But as a gas, one unit of hydrogen takes up 848 times as much space as the same amount in liquid form. Since hydrogen's energy density is so small, it's difficult for vehicles to carry enough gaseous hydrogen to achieve a decent driving range.

To make hydrogen practical, tanks that can store highly pressurized hydrogen gas, which takes up less space, must be developed. Designing such tanks has proved so difficult, however, that some researchers are instead trying to develop ways of storing hydrogen in solid form.

There are consumer barriers behind hydrogen-powered vehicles as well. Many people have concerns that hydrogen is too flammable, and is therefore dangerous as a fuel. Using

There are currently few places to fill up on hydrogen, one barrier to fuel cell vehicles hitting the mass-market.

current technologies, it costs approximately $1 million to build a single FCV. That price is clearly beyond the budget of the average driver. It is also estimated that, for equal amounts of energy, hydrogen costs between two to six times as much as gasoline.[6]

Perhaps the biggest barrier to FCVs is that, as of 2012, there is no practical means of refilling them. It is estimated that it will take at least ten years, and cost hundreds of billions of dollars, to build a hydrogen infrastructure, which supporters call a hydrogen economy, in the United States.

Joseph Romm, a former employee of the US Department of Energy's Office for Energy Efficiency and Renewable Energy, says that before fuel cells can replace gasoline cars, five "miracles" will be required:

1. The cost of the vehicles will have to be reduced.

2. An effective onboard storage system will have to be invented.

3. The cost of producing hydrogen will have to be reduced.

4. An infrastructure will have to be developed.

5. Competing technologies—such as gasoline-powered cars, hybrids, and EVs—will have to stop improving.[7]

As a result, Romm thinks it's very unlikely FCVs will capture more than 5 percent of the vehicle market before 2030.[8]

ICELAND'S HYDROGEN ECONOMY

In Iceland, 93 percent of homes used renewable geothermal energy—energy that is created and stored in the earth in 2006.[9] Icelanders also enjoy easily available hydroelectric power, which is electricity created by running water. These renewable energy sources offer an environmentally friendly way to produce hydrogen, as opposed to using fossil fuels. Iceland therefore made a commitment in 2009 to switch to a hydrogen economy, where almost all fuel needs will be met by using hydrogen. They already have fuel-cell-powered buses and public filling stations that produce hydrogen using electrolysis. If all goes as planned, 100 percent of Iceland's vehicles will run on fuel cells by 2040.[10] In recent years, however, there has been speculation as to whether Iceland was pursuing this goal aggressively enough, and whether it was completely feasible.

There's no doubt that a lot of time, money, and work will be required before hydrogen technology reaches the consumer market. But many researchers believe in hydrogen's possibilities and continue to work on innovations to improve fuel cell technology for vehicles. As research continues and innovations are developed in not only hydrogen, but hybrid, electric, and even internal combustion technologies, most experts agree that the future of alternative vehicles looks promising.

CHAPTER 9

DRIVING TOWARD TOMORROW

There are several technological barriers to the future success of all types of alternative vehicles, including high initial costs, high fueling costs, unavailable fuels, limited range, safety, and improvements in the gasoline-powered competition. People's preferences and routines can present barriers that must be overcome as well.

Some green technologies have little direct impact on a person's daily routine. A home or business using electricity from a renewable utility grid will likely function in much the same way as those that receive electricity from a grid powered by a coal-burning plant. A car, however, is a tangible object used every day that can represent who a person is and how he or she lives. This is why alternative vehicles cannot succeed unless drivers accept them. And unfortunately, that acceptance has been slow in coming.

« For alternative vehicles to truly take off, their maintenance must be easily adaptable to people's everyday lives.

Some people believe that trying to change the vehicles we drive is pointless, as car emissions create only a fraction of the world's pollution problem. More often, however, people resist change because they do not believe alternative vehicles can meet their performance needs on the road. According to Curtis and Judy Anderson, authors of *Electric and Hybrid Cars: A History*, if people are given the choice between fuel economy and acceleration, they always choose acceleration.[1] Fortunately, with the new alternative vehicles already on the market and those currently being developed, it is often not necessary to choose.

Good performance is not enough, however. As one team of researchers stated in a *Journal of Power Sources* article, "Any new technology which aspires to compete with an existing technology will only succeed if it matches, or preferably exceeds, the state-of-art at the same, or preferably lower, cost."[2]

Scientists are working to make alternative vehicles less expensive to purchase. In the

SUPERIOR TO STONES

Despite many clean innovations, approximately 97 percent of all energy consumed by vehicles today still comes from dwindling fossil fuel reserves.[3] But scientists and engineers remain optimistic. "The stone age didn't end because we ran out of stones," says Larry Burns, director of The Earth Institute's Roundtable on Sustainable Mobility. "Superior technology can replace a proven one by offering advantages rather than by waiting for a resource to run out."[4]

meantime, it is important to recognize that green vehicles can be less expensive to own. For example, if gasoline cost only $2.50 per gallon, it would be nearly a dollar less than prices in 2012. Over one year, it would take $1,172 to refuel a medium-sized ICE car, approximately $750 to fuel and charge a similarly sized HEV, and $371 to charge a pure EV. A PHEV would cost approximately $400 to fuel and charge annually.[5]

And what about the range problem posed by electric power? A limited driving range is unappealing for many consumers, but the truth is this problem may not ever actually come into play. According to the National Resources Defense Council Staff blog, as of 2011, the average American drives less than 40 miles (64 km) per day.[6] Some electric vehicles currently for sale in North America, such as the Nissan Leaf EV, are designed to drive a range of 100 miles (161 km). And Tesla vehicles are designed to go as far as 300 miles (483 km) per charge.

The challenge is getting the electric energy into the electric vehicle. The charging infrastructure for these long-range vehicles requires much higher power than conventional electric systems can deliver. Therefore, a new electric grid and high power plants to generate such power would have to be constructed in order for these long-range electric vehicles to really take off.

NEW HORIZONS

What energy sources will carmakers harness next? Solar power is one option.

Solar panels create electricity for homes and businesses, and it's already possible to refuel an electric vehicle by plugging it into a solar-powered charging station. But why stop there? Since the 1970s, researchers have been experimenting with vehicles that have solar panels built right in. There are no such cars available for consumer purchase today, but many test models have already been developed.

Solar panels turn sunlight into electricity, and the amount produced depends on the intensity of the light: the sunnier the day, the more electricity will be produced. Solar panels have a natural limit, and that limit cannot be increased. Therefore, to use solar power for vehicles, engineers have to design cars that can operate within that limit. Solar cars must be lightweight and very efficient, have low aerodynamic drag, and have a low rolling resistance. It also helps if the onboard solar panels can swivel to catch the sun as it changes positions.

Hybrid solar electric vehicles use two power sources: an electric motor and a solar panel that charges the batteries with sunlight as the second source of power rather than gasoline. Using sunlight instead of gasoline turns solar-assisted models into zero-emissions vehicles. Looking at it in another way, batteries can assist a solar-powered car by storing electricity for driving the car at night.

A prototype vehicle
with solar panels
covering the roof

Solar-electric vehicles are still very expensive, and at the moment they are only truly workable in areas that reliably receive lots of sunshine. And as with other types of alternative vehicles, cost and range are also issues. But some carmakers are starting to incorporate small solar panels into conventional car models. For example, the Nissan Leaf SL has solar panels in the rear spoiler that help charge its small starting battery.

Another future alternative may be solar PHEV vehicles powered by a combination of electricity from solar panels and biofuel. Frank has calculated that such a car would need approximately 200 square feet (19 sq m) of today's solar panels and only the ethanol of today's reformulated gasoline to create a completely green vehicle for the masses.[9] However, cost is still currently a barrier in these technologies.

Some believe the ultimate vehicle technology has not even been thought of yet. Instead of thinking about cars that create as few emissions as possible, Donald Sadoway, head of the Extreme Electrochemistry group at the Massachusetts Institute of Technology says, think about cars that could actually *clean the air* as they drive. "Today we're at a negative, and the best we can hope to achieve is to get as close to zero, but . . . . Why can't you bust through the zero axis and go positive?" he asks.[10] Whether as cars that are cleaner for the air or cars that actually *clean* the air, the future of alternative vehicles promises to be an exciting race of innovative ideas.

ALGAE POWER

In 2009, a car that ran on a type of fuel never used before was unveiled in San Francisco. Made by the Sapphire Energy company, the Algaeus hybrid used an electric motor teamed with a biofuel engine powered by algae. The Algaeus, built into the shell of a Prius, was touted as getting approximately 150 miles per gallon (53 km/L) in PHEV mode on a ten-day tour across the nation upon being revealed to the public.[11] The algae used to create the vehicle's fuel is grown in saltwater ponds onsite at Sapphire Energy's facility.

GLOSSARY

AERODYNAMIC DRAG—The friction caused by wind hitting a moving object, such as a vehicle.

CARBON CYCLE—The pathway a carbon atom follows from fuel to vehicle to atmosphere and back to fuel.

CHEMICAL ENERGY—Energy released by a chemical reaction.

EFFICIENCY—The percentage of energy found in a fuel that is ultimately converted to a vehicle's motion.

ELECTROMAGNET—A piece of iron that becomes a magnet when an electric current passes through wire coiled around it.

EMISSIONS—The waste molecules that make up a vehicle's exhaust. They may include greenhouse gases and/or other harmful pollutants.

ENERGY DENSITY—The energy something has relative to its volume or size.

FLEX-FUEL VEHICLE—A vehicle with an internal combustion engine that can use more than one type of fuel or a fuel blend.

FOOT-AND-MOUTH DISEASE—A highly contagious virus that causes fever and blisters on the feet and mouth that can be contracted by humans.

FUEL ECONOMY—The measure of how many miles a vehicle can travel using one gallon of fuel, usually gasoline or diesel.

GAME THEORY—The study of complex interactions and decision-making processes such as those involved in playing games.

MECHANICAL ENERGY—Energy of a physical system in motion and doing work.

NANOTECHNOLOGY—The science of very tiny things.

NEUROBIOLOGY—Brain science.

REFORMING—A method of producing hydrogen gas from hydrocarbons such as gasoline or methanol.

REFORMULATED GASOLINE—A blend of fossil fuel gasoline and ethanol.

ROLLING RESISTANCE—The friction between the moving tires of a vehicle and the road.

SPECIFIC ENERGY—The energy something has relative to its weight.

STATE OF CHARGE—The amount of electric energy remaining in a battery, expressed as a percentage of the battery's total capacity.

VOLTAGE—A measure of electric pressure, which is created by the difference in charge between a battery's anode and cathode.

ADDITIONAL RESOURCES

SELECTED BIBLIOGRAPHY

Anderson, Curtis D., and Judy Anderson. *Electric and Hybrid Cars: A History*. 2nd ed. Jefferson, NC: McFarland, 2010. Print.

Chan, C. C. "The State of the Art of Electric, Hybrid, and Fuel Cell Vehicles." *Proceedings of the Institute of Electrical and Electronics Engineers* 95.4 (2007): 704–718. Print.

Chiras, Dan. *Green Transportation Basics*. Gabriola Island, BC: New Society, 2010. Print.

Romm, Joseph. "The Car and Fuel of the Future." *Energy Policy* 34 (2006): 2,609–2,614. Print.

FURTHER READINGS

Conley, Robin. *Inventions That Shaped the World: The Automobile*. New York: Franklin Watts, 2005. Print.

Harper, Gavin D. J. *Fuel Cell Projects for the Evil Genius*. New York: McGraw-Hill, 2008. Print.

MacKay, Jennifer. *Technology 360: Electric Cars*. Farmington Hills, MI: Lucent, 2011. Print.

WEB LINKS

To learn more about hybrid and electric vehicles, visit ABDO Publishing Company online at **www.abdopublishing.com**. Web sites about hybrid and electric vehicles are featured on our Book Links page. These links are routinely monitored and updated to provide the most current information available.

FOR MORE INFORMATION

For more information on this subject, contact or visit the following organizations:

US DEPARTMENT OF ENERGY ALTERNATIVE FUELS & ADVANCED VEHICLES DATA CENTER
http://www.afdc.energy.gov/

This organization promotes the use of vehicle and fuel innovations and alternatives and gathers information on ways to reduce oil dependency and use in the United States.

US ENVIRONMENTAL PROTECTION AGENCY
1200 Pennsylvania Avenue, NW, Washington, DC 20460
202-272-0167
http://www.epa.gov

An organization dedicated to providing research and information on all aspects of environmental concern. Contact the EPA for more information on air quality, vehicle emissions, and green vehicles.

SOURCE NOTES

CHAPTER 1. RUNNING ON FUMES

1. Pieter Tans. "Trends in Atmospheric Carbon Dioxide." *NOAA Earth System Research Laboratory Global Monitoring Division*. US Department of Commerce, NOAA, 7 May 2012. Web. 20 Aug. 2012.

2. Edward Humes. *Eco Barons: The Dreamers, Schemers, and Millionaires Who Are Saving Our Planet*. New York: HarperCollins, 2009. Print. 298.

3. Curtis D. Anderson and Judy Anderson. *Electric and Hybrid Cars: A History*. 2nd ed. Jefferson, NC: McFarland, 2010. Print. 109.

4. "2041: No Oil, No Replacement." *UC Davis News and Information*. University of California-Davis, 17 Nov. 2010. Web. 29 Aug. 2012.

5. Edward Humes. *Eco Barons: The Dreamers, Schemers, and Millionaires Who Are Saving Our Planet*. New York: HarperCollins, 2009. Print. 12.

6. Curtis D. Anderson and Judy Anderson. *Electric and Hybrid Cars: A History*. 2nd ed. Jefferson, NC: McFarland, 2010. Print. 107.

7. Sherry Boschert. *Plug-In Hybrids: The Cars That Will Recharge America*. Gabriola Island, BC: New Society, 2006. Print. 150.

8. Edward Humes. *Eco Barons: The Dreamers, Schemers, and Millionaires Who Are Saving Our Planet*. New York: HarperCollins, 2009. Print. 242.

CHAPTER 2. THE HORSELESS CARRIAGE

1. Curtis D. Anderson and Judy Anderson. *Electric and Hybrid Cars: A History*. 2nd ed. Jefferson, NC: McFarland, 2010. Print. 111.

2. Ibid. 112.

3. Ibid. 22.

4. Hannah Elliott. "In Photos: Edison's Electric Cars, Circa 1900." *Forbes*. Forbes.com, 11 Oct. 2010. Web. 29 Aug. 2012.

5. Curtis D. Anderson and Judy Anderson. *Electric and Hybrid Cars: A History*. 2nd ed. Jefferson, NC: McFarland, 2010. Print. 173.

6. Ibid. 194.

7. "Events of the Day in the World of Sport: First Automobile Fifty-Mile Race Ever Run in America." *New York Times*. New York Times, 15 Apr. 1900. Web. 29 Aug. 2012.

8. Ernest H. Wakefield. *History of the Electric Automobile: Battery-Only Powered Cars*. Warrendale, PA: Society of Automotive Engineers, 1994. Print. 237.

9. Curtis D. Anderson and Judy Anderson. *Electric and Hybrid Cars: A History*. 2nd ed. Jefferson, NC: McFarland, 2010. Print. 37.

10. *Car: The Definitive Visual History of the Automobile*. New York: DK, 2011. *Google Book Search*. Web. 29 Aug. 2012.

11. Sherry Boschert. *Plug-In Hybrids: The Cars That Will Recharge America*. Gabriola Island, BC: New Society, 2006. Print. 139–40.

12. Seth Fletcher. *Bottled Lightning: Superbatteries, Electric Cars, and the New Lithium Economy*. New York: Farrar, 2011. Print. 117.

CHAPTER 3. INTERNAL COMBUSTION ENGINE VEHICLES

1. M. Contestabile, G. J. Offer, R. Slade, F. Jaeger, and M. Thoennes. "Battery Electric Vehicles, Hydrogen Fuel Cells and Biofuels. Which Will Be the Winner?" *Energy & Environment Science* 4 (2011): 3758. Print.

2. Curtis D. Anderson and Judy Anderson. *Electric and Hybrid Cars: A History*. 2nd ed. Jefferson, NC: McFarland, 2010. Print. 135.

3. Erica Werner. "EPA Proposing Limits on Emissions From Lawn Mowers." *Seattle Times*. Seattle Times, 13 Jun. 2008. Web. 29 Aug. 2012.

4. Cathy Milbourn. "EPA Tightens Engine Standards on Surf and Turf." *EPA Newsroom*. US EPA, 4 Sep. 2008. Web. 29 Aug. 2012.

5. Curtis D. Anderson and Judy Anderson. *Electric and Hybrid Cars: A History*. 2nd ed. Jefferson, NC: McFarland, 2010. Print. 21.

6. Ibid. 124.

7. Dan Chiras. *Green Transportation Basics*. Gabriola Island, BC: New Society, 2010. Print. 157–163.

8. Curtis D. Anderson and Judy Anderson. *Electric and Hybrid Cars: A History*. 2nd ed. Jefferson, NC: McFarland, 2010. Print. 159.

9. Ernest H. Wakefield. *History of the Electric Automobile: Hybrid Electric Vehicles*. Warrendale, PA: Society of Automotive Engineers, 1998. Print. 19.

CHAPTER 4. ELECTRIC VEHICLES

1. Curtis D. Anderson and Judy Anderson. *Electric and Hybrid Cars: A History*. 2nd ed. Jefferson, NC: McFarland, 2010. Print. 12.

2. Ernest H. Wakefield. *History of the Electric Automobile: Hybrid Electric Vehicles*. Warrendale, PA: Society of Automotive Engineers, 1998. Print. 19.

3. Seth Fletcher. *Bottled Lightning: Superbatteries, Electric Cars, and the New Lithium Economy*. New York: Farrar, 2011. Print. Epigraph.

4. Ibid. 78.

5. Ibid. 111.

6. Eric J. Leech. "Regenerative Braking . . . The Stop 'n' Go Money Saver." *HowStuffWorks*. HowStuffWorks, n.d. Web. 29 Aug. 2012.

7. Curtis D. Anderson and Judy Anderson. *Electric and Hybrid Cars: A History*. 2nd ed. Jefferson, NC: McFarland, 2010. Print. 126.

8. *Who Killed the Electric Car?* Dir. Chris Paine. Sony Pictures Classics, 2006. DVD.

9. Curtis D. Anderson and Judy Anderson. *Electric and Hybrid Cars: A History*. 2nd ed. Jefferson, NC: McFarland, 2010. Print. 126.

10. "What Happens Next to Car Batteries." *Earth911. com*. Earth911.com, 2012. Web. 29 Aug. 2012.

CHAPTER 5. HYBRIDS

1. Stuart Lavietes. "Victor Wouk, 86, Dies; Built Early Hybrid Car." *New York Times*. New York Times, 12 Jun. 2005. Web. 29 Aug. 2012.

2. C. C. Chan. "The State of the Art of Electric, Hybrid, and Fuel Cell Vehicles." *Proceedings of the Institute of Electrical and Electronics Engineers* 95.4 (2007): 706. Print.

3. Jack Erjavec. *Automotive Technology: A Systems Approach*. 5th ed. Independence, KY: Delmar Cengage Learning, 2009. *Google Book Search*. Web. 29 Aug. 2012.

4. "Lowered Emissions." *Toyota.ca: Benefits of Hybrid Technology*. Toyota Canada, n.d. Web. 29 Aug. 2012.

5. "Compare Side-by-Side." *FuelEconomy.gov*. US Department of Energy, n.d. Web. 14 July 2012.

CHAPTER 6. PLUG-IN HYBRID ELECTRIC VEHICLES

1. Alysha Webb. "The Electrifying Rebels." *Automotive News*. Crain Communications, 29 Nov. 2010. Web. 30 Aug. 2012.

2. Tom Clynes. "The Energy Fix: 10 Steps to End America's Fossil-Fuel Addiction." *Popular Science* 1 July 2006. *EBSCO Megafile*. Web. 31 Aug. 2012.

3. S. B. Han, Y. H. Chang, Y. J. Chung, E. Y. Lee, B. Suh, and A. Frank. "Fuel Economy Comparison of Conventional Drive Trains Series and Parallel Hybrid Electric Step Vans." *International Journal of Automotive Technology* 10.2(2009): 235–240. Print.

4. Chris Walsh, Steve Carroll, Andy Easlake, and Phil Blythe. *Electric Vehicle Driving Style and Duty Variation Performance Study*. Cenex, Nov. 2010. Print. 10.

5. Dan Chiras. *Green Transportation Basics*. Gabriola Island, BC: New Society, 2010. Print. 60–62.

6. Shaik Amjad, S. Neelakrishnan, and R. Rudramoorthy. "Review of Design Considerations and Technological Challenges for Successful Development and Deployment of Plug-In Hybrid Electric Vehicles." *Renewable and Sustainable Energy Reviews* 14 (2010): 1105. Print.

7. "Chevrolet Volt Saves Supertanker of Gas." *GM News*. General Motors, 17 May 2012. Web. 31 Aug. 2012.

8. S. B. Han, Y. H. Chang, Y. J. Chung, E. Y. Lee, B. Suh, and A. Frank. "Fuel Economy Comparison of Conventional Drive Trains Series and Parallel Hybrid Electric Step Vans." *International Journal of Automotive Technology* 10.2(2009): 235–240. Print.

CHAPTER 7. LITHIUM BATTERIES: PROMISE AND PERIL

1. "Meeting of the American Institute of Electrical Engineers." *The Electrical World* 23 Jan. 1897. *Google Book Search*. Web. 31 Aug. 2012.

2. Seth Fletcher. *Bottled Lightning: Superbatteries, Electric Cars, and the New Lithium Economy*. New York: Farrar, 2011. Print. 60–61.

3. "Increasing Energy Density Means Increasing Range." *Tesla*. Tesla, n.d. Web. 30 Aug. 2012.

4. Seth Fletcher. *Bottled Lightning: Superbatteries, Electric Cars, and the New Lithium Economy*. New York: Farrar, 2011. Print. 16–17.

5. Ibid.

6. Ibid. 131.

7. Ibid. 146.

8. Ibid. 84.

9. Fred Durso Jr. "Elemental Questions." *National Fire Protection Association*. National Fire Protection Association, Mar./Apr. 2012. Web. 30 Aug. 2012.

10. "Chevrolet Volt Fire Roars, Fizzles." *MotorSpaceNW.com*. Spokesman-Review, 2012. Web. 31 Aug. 2012.

11. Chuck Squatriglia. "GM Defends Chevy Volt Following Post-Crash Fires." *Wired*. Condé Nast, 28 Nov. 2011. Web. 30 Aug. 2012.

12. Juchuan Li, Fuqian Yang, Jia Ye, and Yang-Tse Cheng. "Whisker Formation on a Thin Film Tin Lithium-Ion Battery Anode." *Journal of Power Sources* 196(2011): 1476. Print.

13. Seth Fletcher. *Bottled Lightning: Superbatteries, Electric Cars, and the New Lithium Economy*. New York: Farrar, 2011. Print. 197.

CHAPTER 8. FUEL CELL VEHICLES

1. Sherry Boschert. *Plug-In Hybrids: The Cars That Will Recharge America*. Gabriola Island, BC: New Society, 2006. Print. 58–59.

2. "Natural Gas Reforming." *US Department of Energy: Energy Efficiency & Renewable Energy*. US Department of Energy, 8 Mar. 2011. Web. 30 Aug. 2012.

3. Joseph Romm. "California's Hydrogen Highway Reconsidered." *Digital Commons*. Golden Gate University School of Law, 10 Jan. 2010. Web. 31 Aug. 2012.

4. Mitch Vine. "Ballard Power: Great Karma But Poor Investment." *Seeking Alpha*. Seeking Alpha, 2 Sept. 2011. Web. 30 Aug. 2012.

5. Curtis D. Anderson and Judy Anderson. *Electric and Hybrid Cars: A History*. 2nd ed. Jefferson, NC: McFarland, 2010. Print. 55.

6. B. D. McNicol, D. A. J. Rand, and K. R. Williams. "Fuel Cells For Road Transportation Purposes—Yes or No?" *Journal of Power Sources* 100 (2001): 54. Print.

7. *Who Killed the Electric Car?* Dir. Chris Paine. Sony Pictures Classics, 2006. DVD.

8. Joseph Romm. "The Car and Fuel of the Future." *Energy Policy* 34 (2006): 2611. Print.

9. Lester R. Brown. "Plan B 2.0: Rescuing a Planet Under Stress and a Civilization in Trouble." *Earth Policy Institute*. Earth Policy Institute, n. d. Web. 30 Aug. 2012.

10. Tom Clynes. "The Energy Fix: 10 Steps to End America's Fossil-Fuel Addiction." *Popular Science* 1 July 2006. *EBSCO Megafile*. Web. 31 Aug. 2012.

CHAPTER 9. DRIVING TOWARD TOMORROW

1. Curtis D. Anderson and Judy Anderson. *Electric and Hybrid Cars: A History*. 2nd ed. Jefferson, NC: McFarland, 2010. Print. 106.

2. B. D. McNicol, D. A. J. Rand, and K. R. Williams. "Fuel Cells For Road Transportation Purposes—Yes or No?" *Journal of Power Sources* 100(2001): 58. Print.

3. Liza Barth. "Average Gas Prices—December 12, 2011." *Consumer Reports*. Consumers Union of US. 12 Dec. 2011. Web. 30 Aug. 2012.

4. Curtis D. Anderson and Judy Anderson. *Electric and Hybrid Cars: A History*. 2nd ed. Jefferson, NC: McFarland, 2010. Print. 231.

5. Sherry Boschert. *Plug-In Hybrids: The Cars That Will Recharge America*. Gabriola Island, BC: New Society, 2006. Print. 39.

6. Max Baumhefner. "Get it Right USA Today—Americans Want Electric Cars." *Switchboard*. Natural Defense Council, 25 May 2011. Web. 30 Aug. 2012.

7. Ernest H. Wakefield. *History of the Electric Automobile: Hybrid Electric Vehicles*. Warrendale, PA: Society of Automotive Engineers, 1998. Print. 237.

8. Ibid. 210.

9. Dane Muldoon. "Interview with Prof. Andrew Frank, Head of the UC-Davis Challenge X Entry, Team Fate." *AutoBlogGreen*. AOL, 29 Mar. 2007. Web. 30 Aug. 2012.

10. Seth Fletcher. *Bottled Lightning: Superbatteries, Electric Cars, and the New Lithium Economy*. New York: Farrar, 2011. Print. 195.

11. "Algae-Fueled Car Completes 3,750 Mile Cross Country Tour." *Sapphire Energy*. Sapphire Energy, 18 Sept. 2009. Web. 30 Aug. 2012.

INDEX

ABOUT THE AUTHOR

In 2006, L. E. Carmichael won the Governor General's Award for her PhD thesis, *Ecological Genetics of Northern Wolves and Arctic Foxes*. These days, she writes for children and teenagers instead of other scientists. Carmichael's articles have appeared in magazines like *Kiki*, *Relate*, and *Highlights for Children*. She's also a regular contributor to the Canadian children's science writers' blog *Sci/Why*. Children's books she has authored include *Humpback Whale Migration*, *Locust Migration*, and *Wildebeest Migration*.

ABOUT THE CONTENT CONSULTANT

Professor Andrew Frank is a professor of Mechanical and Aeronautical Engineering at the University of California, Davis. His areas of interest include mechanical design and control systems, mechanical transmission systems including the Continuously Variable Transmission or CVT, transportation systems, ICEs and PHEVs. Frank has researched and invented innovations for all types of vehicles, but his main focus has been PHEVs. Many regard Frank as the father of the modern PHEV. He holds more than 35 patents, 12 of them belonging to the University of California, Davis, all relating to alternative vehicle technology. Frank also is the CTO of Efficient Drivetrains Inc., a company that provides the professionals in the vehicle industry innovative products, services, and support.